"The men of Issachar were the military scou[ts?]
God was doing through His people, but also understood what the enemy was up to and were able to report to God's people God's strategy for that season. Stuart Simpson, a friend and co-worker in Christ's kingdom, is such a man today. Having lived as a missionary with his wonderful family in three continents, and especially with his China experience, the author has a global perspective which he passes on to the reader in an interesting, informative, concise, yet powerful way in his book, *Empowered!* It's a "must read book" for all who want to see Christ's Great Commission finished in this generation."

LOREN CUNNINGHAM

Co-founder, Youth With A Mission

"I love this book! Stuart Simpson's new book, *Empowered! Discovering Your Place in God's Story*, is a must read for every follower of Jesus who is serious about their walk with God. Stuart gives God's blueprint for each of us to find our place in fulfilling our God-given assignment as part of God's agenda, the Great Commission. *Empowered!* shows us practically how every believer and every local community (church) of believers need to become missional in the way we live our lives. The truths in this book will change the world!"

LARRY KREIDER

DOVE International Director and author of over 30 books

"Empowered! is more than a "must read" for those interested in God's purpose for ALL His people. It should be a book study in every evangelistically conscious and/or kingdom-oriented local church, and a text for students who want to understand God's mission in our world. A thoughtful and scripturally-based proposal for what Stuart Simpson calls the 'Fourth Wave'."

BOB MOFFITT

President, Harvest Foundation;
Co-Founder of the Disciple Nations Alliance

"Empowered! provides us with a thoroughly stimulating guide to help the church re-align itself around God's eternal purposes in Jesus. Written with the view to world missions, it is applicable to the Western church as well. A good read."

ALAN HIRSCH

Thought Leader & Key Mission Strategist

"Stuart Simpson has provided us with a sweeping, cobweb-clearing vision of the ongoing movement of God, not only in the past, but as it is presently unfolding. Christians in what is wrongly called "secular work," local church leaders, and mission boards need to let the message of this book disrupt traditional categories and point the way down a path so old it seems new."

LARRY PEABODY

Author of *Serving Christ in the Workplace* and
Job-Shadowing Daniel: Walking the Talk at Work

"*Empowered!* reflects the massive paradigm shifts in the global church, the peoples still to be reached, and methods and models of how to see effective mission and kingdom transformation. Stuart's insights are timely and highly relevant for everyone who wants to see all nations discipled and to engage the whole Church in mission. We are living in a time of huge change and reading *Empowered!* will both inspire and challenge you. For some it may raise some uncomfortable questions, while for others it will be a huge encouragement and endorsement of new ways of being church and of doing mission. I will be recommending it as a "must read" to everyone involved in Kairos around the world."

LINDA HARDING

International Executive Director of Kairos International;
European Director of World Outreach

"Stuart Simpson's book, *Empowered! Discovering Your Place in God's Story,* is pointing both Christians who are committed to missions and the larger church to the future of the Church's engagement in the world. Missions are changing. There is a growing frustration among global Christians; they are asking: "Is this all there is to the church and to the Christian life?" The answer to the question is a resounding "No!" There is more! The more is a comprehensive vision that involves every Christian in every area of their lives. The summons to mission is every Christian's call. The God of the universe wants to advance his kingdom through the work of each and every Christian. Simpson's book shows us the Fourth Wave."

DARROW MILLER

Co-Founder, Disciple Nations Alliance;
Author of *LifeWork: A Biblical Theology for What You Do Every Day*

"I have read this book with great interest and feel there will be many like it over the next ten years. This is a forerunner document alerting the Body of Christ to the reality that a new way of doing things is imminent, if not already upon us. Content like this will serve to legitimize what now is considered to be experimental or outside the mainstream of acceptable strategy."

TOM HALLAS

Pacific & Asia Field Director, Youth With A Mission

"The Great Commission is the mandate of God given to all Christians since the first coming of Christ. This book serves as a timely reminder to all that every Christian has a part to play to reach the world for Jesus. *Empowered!* by Stuart Simpson gives the reader a background of how evangelism has evolved through the years. It seeks to redefine missions, expanding the responsibility of evangelism to include EVERYONE! Empowered! is what all Christians should be to fulfill the calling of God in our lives!"

KONG HEE

City Harvest Church, Singapore

"This is not your ordinary book on missions, or evangelism, or finding one's calling. It's a combination of all three. Starting with a historical overview of modern missions and flowing out of his first-hand experience along with practical tools for finding one's place in God's work, Simpson brings us up-to-date with *Empowered!* for missional living today."

KEITH E. WEBB

Author, *The COACH Model for Christian Leaders*;
Principal of Creative Results Management

"*Empowered!* steps into a fresh evaluation of our present history and invites God's people to walk with the integrity of ambassadors of a kingdom that is present in society, within us as priests and coming in fullness."

DAVID COLLINS

Founder Food for the Hungry Canada and Paradigm Ministries

"The first thing you need to know about this book is that it comes from an author with extensive mission experience. Not long ago, I heard a respected author and speaker say that they only read books from people who have lived what they are writing about. It's evident from this book that the author speaks from his own experience and life journey. The book has three main parts: **God's Story:** a biblical picture of God's mission & kingdom, and how this has shaped, or not, society and the Church; **Every Believer's Story:** through the Church, God calls, commissions and equips all His people for mission; **Engaging with God's Story:** a deeper look at finding God's specific purposes for your life and ministry. The main theme that comes across from the book, and this is a major reason why you should read it, is that our individual calling doesn't begin with us, but with God and the outworking of His purposes. This is the key to an empowered and fulfilling life. It's a very easy to read and practical book, with an appendix of tools to help you, including spiritual gifts questionnaires, personality tests and study questions. This makes it a great workbook for anyone wanting to explore and work through God's call on their lives.

MIKE FRITH

Founding Director, OSCAR Mission Resources

"This book addresses the needs for the global church; speaking hope and warning the body of Christ. It clearly explains God's greater mission and spells out where every child of God fits in the greater picture. It satisfies the keen mind and the seeking heart and it is useful to all members in the body of Christ irrespective of office or gifting. If you've ever felt your job is drawing you away from God, this book will help you advance God's Kingdom at your workplace."

Dr. GIVEMORE SAKUHUNI
University Lecturer, Metallurgist, African

"In this book, Stuart Simpson calls us to attend to the biggest possible picture and embark on the greatest adventure there is to be a part of, namely, the Kingdom of God! Whilst Jesus spoke of 'church' on a couple of occasions, He described the Kingdom of Heaven over one hundred times. As disciples of Jesus, is our focus the same as our Master's? Whilst there have been many waves of mission, Stuart describes a 'fourth wave' including ideas such as simple/organic/missional house church, business as mission and discipling nations through equipping the saints to bring Kingdom principles and practices into the spheres of society. For those who want to be part of what our King is doing in our generation...I wholeheartedly recommend reading this book...but be prepared, as a disciple of Jesus, you will want to get in on the action as a result."

PETER J. FARMER
Founder of Mission Britain & Newforms Resources;
Co-author, Pioneer Mission & Kingdom Mission

EMPOWERED!

DISCOVERING YOUR PLACE IN GOD'S STORY

EMPOWERED!

DISCOVERING YOUR PLACE IN GOD'S STORY

STUART SIMPSON

Catalyst Ministries
Stimulating Action & Effecting Change

EMPOWERED!

Copyright © 2013, 2019 by Stuart M. Simpson

www.catalystmin.org

Published by Catalyst Ministries

Second Printing

All rights reserved. No part of this book may be reproduced in any form without permission in writing from the author, except in the case of brief excerpts for review purposes.

The website addresses recommended at the end of this book are offered as a resource to you. These websites are not intended in any way to be or imply an endorsement on behalf of Catalyst Ministries, nor do we vouch for their content.

ISBN: 978-1-291-54000-0

Unless otherwise indicated, Scripture quotations are taken from the Holy Bible, New Kings James Version, Copyright © 1979, 1980, 1982 by Thomas Nelson, Inc., Publishers.

Dedication

This book is dedicated to *every* believer who has always wanted to contribute to God's mission in the world but never knew if, and how, they could. My hope is that this book will show you that you can, and provide you with some tools to get you started in discovering your place in God's story.

Contents

Introduction   3

Part 1: God's Story   7

Chapter 1: Framing the Story

Chapter 2: Faulty Story Paradigms

Chapter 3: The Big Story of God's Kingdom

Chapter 4: The Transforming Story of God's Kingdom

Part 2: Every Believer's Story   93

Chapter 5: The Missional Nature of the Church

Chapter 6: The Calling of Every Believer

Chapter 7: The Commissioning of Every Believer

Chapter 8: The Equipping of Every Believer

Part 3: Engaging with God's Story   165

Chapter 9: What Are *You* Living For?

Chapter 10: Discovering Your Unique Role in God's Kingdom Mission

Chapter 11: Intentional Action

Conclusion   209

Appendix: Tools to Help You Understand How God Has Made You   223

Bibliography   255

Additional Resources   263

Questions for Reflection and Discussion   265

About the Author   273

Acknowledgements

The idea for this book began while I was listening to YWAM's Pacific & Asia Field Director, Tom Hallas, share with a group of YWAM Discipleship Training School students in Thailand in 2008. As he was sharing about a new 'Fourth Wave of Missions' and referring to a recent YWAM publication on bringing God's kingdom to earth through the discipling of nations, it occurred to me that as good as this book was, it would probably not appeal to, or reach the hands of, most 'ordinary' Christian believers. Sensing that God was encouraging me to write a book that would, and that was directed towards embracing *every* believer, I started a writing project that would take four to five years to complete. Two publishers were willing to take on my book but as I was unable to come up with the necessary author financial contribution towards the initial print-run, I decided to go ahead with publishing it myself. The book manuscript simply remaining on my laptop wasn't going to empower anyone!

As with any writing project of this kind I am indebted to the help of a number of other people. Thank you, Tom, for being the catalyst God used to drop the idea of this book into my heart; Darrow Miller for investing your time and wisdom in helping me to get free from certain unbiblical paradigms of thinking, and for your valuable contributions and feedback; Ryan Davis for your excellent editorial suggestions which have made this a more empowering book; Loren Cunningham for your personal encouragement that I had something significant to write; and to my wife, Michelle, for always sharpening my arrow and for your endless patience as I've tapped away to try and get this first major writing project finished. Finally, thank you Jesus for giving me eyes to see so that I can help 'clean other people's windows.'

Introduction

Surveys in the United States indicate that most Christians feel disempowered.[1] There are reasons for this. A lack of teaching that releases people to identify and then pursue their God-given gifting. An end-times perspective that results in believers resigned to the way things are and biding their time, waiting for the Rapture or Jesus' Second Coming to rescue them out of this world's mess.[2] Wrong thinking that separates the whole of life into two different categories: what is spiritual and really important, and what is material or secular and less important. This results in a division within the church between the clergy and the laity, those in "full-time Christian ministry" and those who are not. Such thinking has robbed many believers of the joy of knowing their life can make a difference.

The purpose of this book is to help give *every* Christian believer the realization that they have a special, God-given role and place in the fulfillment of God's mission on earth. God is writing a story in which he invites each one of us to participate. This book will help you to engage and live out your story within God's story and mission. It may seem obvious to many Christians, but in looking at the unique human role and contribution to that mission, we will revisit and explore what the Great Commission is.

---

[1] Os Hillman, www.marketplaceleaders.org.
[2] Vishal Mangalwadi refers to this as an "eschatological paralysis" in his book *Truth and Transformation: A Manifesto for Ailing Nations* (Seattle: YWAM Publishing, 2009), 213.

> "All authority has been given to me in heaven and on earth. Go therefore and make disciples of all the nations, baptizing them in the name of the Father and of the Son and of the Holy Spirit, teaching them to obey all that I have commanded you; and lo, I am with you always, even to the end of the age."
> Jesus (Matthew 28:18–20)

The Great Commission. Ask Christian believers what comes to mind when they read or hear these words and my guess is that many times feelings of guilt, inadequacy, and failure will surface. All sorts of images also probably come into view based on a perception of what they think the Great Commission is all about. "Isn't this what the really spiritual Christians invest their time in? Isn't it for those with evangelistic giftings, or those who have received a special calling to go to China, India, or Timbuktu?" Here's a question for you: What response or reaction do *you* experience when you read or hear these three words?

You may be surprised to discover that your understanding of the Great Commission is too limited. It will become clear that this task is not just for church workers or overseas missionaries. Whatever your vocation in life, you have a destiny to fulfill and a unique contribution to make. My hope is that this book will help you realize how. This book is not intended for scholars, theologians, or missionary practitioners but for the "ordinary" follower of Jesus Christ.

After considering in the first chapter how we view history and especially in the light of the unfolding of God's story, we will discover how, I believe, God wants to *mobilize the whole body of Christ*—the global Church—in a way that will breathe new life, vision, and purpose into every member. What is exciting is that God is inviting *each one of us* to join him in his story and mission to carry the knowledge of the glory of God to every place and every sphere and area of life.

The days in which we currently live are significant days, and it is important we have a sense of purpose of what God is doing in the earth. In some mission circles today there is talk about an emerging "Fourth Wave," which follows three preceding waves which progressively carried the gospel to those in the coastlands (First Wave), those in the interiors (Second Wave), and then to those hidden and unreached by cultural, language and social barriers (Third Wave). A growing number of Christian leaders around the world believe that God is preparing and providing the wind of the Holy Spirit that will create a Fourth Wave. This will be larger than any "wave" that has come before it and will embrace and impact more people than the previous waves put together. This is the wave that you and I can get involved in, no matter who we are and what our vocation is. It is the wave for *all* to be a part of![3]

We need to be the kind of people who not only "understand the times" from the comfort of our deck-chairs but take up our surf-boards and ride the waves that are

---

[3] For a detailed description of the emerging Fourth Wave, see Ron Boehme, *The Fourth Wave: Taking Your Place in the New Era of Missions* (Seattle: YWAM Publishing, 2011).

being driven by the breath of the Holy Spirit. It will not always be an easy ride, but it will be an adventurous one!

God has always intended that his world be once again flooded not with water but with his love, goodness, and grace. Ultimately, he is working towards restoring all things back to his original intent and purpose . . . a world where everything is how he originally desired it to be. That will only be fully realized at the end of his story, but in the meantime, his church is to be an agent of his kingdom *now*, expressing who God is and demonstrating his ways on earth.

The time is now. Will you be a spectator or a participant? The choice is yours.

Read on and discover how you can be a part of God's story for godly change and transformation.

> "For the earth will be filled with the knowledge of the glory of the Lord, as the waters cover the sea." (Habakkuk 2:14)

Part 1
God's Story

CHAPTER 1
FRAMING THE STORY

How Do You View History?

History. The word itself may tempt some of you to skip past this part of the book, particularly if you found the subject of history to be dull and boring at school. It was for me, and I dropped the subject in favor of geography. However, years later in China, when I started to teach my own children history, my interest grew as I saw each historical period as part of a greater whole. History is not just a random set of events and a record of people's and nations' achievements. If this was all that history was about, it would be of some interest but without any lasting meaning or purpose. However, history sets everything within the wider perspective of what God was doing in the earth. History is *HIS*-story, God's story being carried out through time.

Not everyone views history in this way. Living in another culture quickly helps you appreciate this. After my family moved overseas, I quickly began to realize that people do not think the same way. This can be a daily reminder on the roads in Thailand when all the traffic rules seem to have no relevance at all! Even a red traffic light will not ensure every motorist and motorcyclist will stop. As well as "jumping the lights," some will blatantly proceed through a red light, passing others who have stopped, if they see that there isn't any other traffic coming from another direction (for a few even the presence of other traffic is not a consideration!). As I witness such traffic madness, I often ask myself why some people act in this way? Are they just blatant law-breakers, or do they just perceive things differently? In a lot of cases, I believe it is the latter. It is a different way of thinking which says, "If there's no traffic coming, why wait at the light?" It is thinking based on a different view of life and the world created by the culture they live in. We all wear our own set of cultural spectacles, and in many instances, how we see through them can be very different. If your worldview "glasses" have the correct prescription, then you will see the world accurately. If they are the wrong prescription, your view of the world will be distorted.

What Do You See?

When teaching on successful communication, I normally present this picture as an illustration. You may be familiar with it.[4] Some people see a young woman; others see an old lady. What do you see? The point is both can be seen in spite of the fact that some people can only see one of the ladies. One isn't correct and the other wrong. They are both there. It's just what we see through our own glasses of perceived reality.

---

[4] The picture originates from 1888 in Germany and was first seen publicly on a postcard for the "Anchor Buggy Co." with a caption that reads, "You see my wife, but where is my mother in law?" Source:
http://amazingillusions.blogspot.com/2008/11/old-woman-or-young-lady-illusion.html (accessed 2 February 2010).

The key to how we view life is our worldview. It is at the heart of any culture and affects how we view ourselves, life, and the world. It affects *everything*.[5] It affects how we view history. How a person views history will impact how they view life and how they live it. Our worldview is the window by which we view the world and decide, often subconsciously, what is real and important, or unreal and unimportant.[6]

Differing Worldviews

If you are a Hindu and believe that history is cyclical, that historical events are repeated by consecutive societies, history has no ultimate destiny or goal and is therefore like a story without a conclusion. The recurring cycles mean that there is no ultimate story to tell or universal history to be fulfilled. You will not be motivated to improve your circumstances or transform society. Life is essentially a test of survival until you can "transcend" history and attain your own divinity.[7]

As Buddhism is derived from Hinduism, it too has a cyclical view of time and history. This explains the Buddhist symbol of the wheel. History just continues to repeat itself, largely because of karma, the idea that what

---

[5] Lloyd Kwast has identified four "layers" of culture—behavior, values, beliefs, and worldview—whereby the deeper layers affect and give shape to the outer layers.

[6] From the foreword by Phillip E. Johnson in Nancy Pearcey, *Total Truth: Liberating Christianity from Its Cultural Captivity* (Wheaton, Ill.: Crossway Books, 2004), 11.

[7] The author wishes to acknowledge his inspiration for this part of the chapter came after reading Ron Boehme's blog on the Fourth Wave, posted 1 May 2009 (www.usrenewal.org).

goes around comes around.[8] Life is an endless circle of birth, suffering, and rebirth, and people are reincarnated in higher or lower forms according to what they have done. Once again, the focus tends to be more on escaping from this world, rather than investing in it and making it a better place.[9]

If you are a Muslim, your worldview is based on a utopian belief that Islam will one day dominate the world. For that to come to pass, you will endeavor to do whatever is necessary for everything to be brought under submission to the Qur'an, with sharia law as the governing authority in every nation, culminating in the ultimate triumph of Islam. Evidence of this is already being seen in the United Kingdom, where in 2008, Islamic law was officially adopted in Britain with sharia courts given powers to rule on Muslim civil cases.[10]

If you are a secular humanist, for humankind to have any meaning you must believe that the world will get better as evolution demands progress. Such an unfettered optimistic worldview seems wonderful until the realities of global war and suffering challenge the underlying assumptions (this happened with the onset of World War Two, which resulted in changes to the original *Humanist*

---

[8] A doctrine found in Hinduism and Buddhism.
[9] Having lived in Thailand, I know firsthand the sense of hopelessness this fatalistic worldview produces. For instance, there are numerous children's homes set up by Christians, filled with children who have physical and mental disabilities. They are not there because their families cannot take care of them. Rather, they refuse to care for them, based on a belief that their children's handicaps are due to sins committed in a previous life. To escape from this world of suffering they must therefore be left alone to "work off" their bad karma.
[10] http://www.timesonline.co.uk/tol/comment/faith/article4749183.ece (accessed 1 July 2011).

Manifesto[11]). Similarly, a Communist/Marxist also views history with an evolutionary perspective and believes humankind's history will always develop and progress toward a collectivist revolution and utopia, overthrowing the ruling classes along the way in order that the goal be achieved. Sadly, both atheistic worldviews are dependent upon humankind's ability to bring about such ongoing continuous improvement. Without an acknowledgement of God or the supernatural, man becomes his own savior, working together to form a future global community of peaceful coexistence and perfection. With an increasing rejection in the postmodern West of a sense of truth, what basis will there be for any future hope and purpose? As with animistic worldviews, all that is left is fatalistic despair with history simply becoming nothing more than a point of view.

In a similar vein, the New Age philosophy[12] recognizes no personal God, only a cosmic force (or "the Universe"), and believes that humankind will eventually attain to the heights of goodness, perfection, and "godlikeness," as we all work together to make the world "a better place." Like a fairy tale, ultimately there will be a happy ending.

Essentially, in spite of all the different variations, there are really only three major worldviews:

---

[11] This first public declaration of the humanist worldview was published in 1933.

[12] A revival of Eastern and animistic religion masked in Western language. The New Age has been called "Hinduism in a business suit." (Darrow L. Miller, *Discipling the Nations: The Power of Truth to Transform Cultures* (Seattle: YWAM Publishing, 1998).

- *Secularism* (or secular humanism): the atheistic belief that there is no God or spiritual dimension; the predominant worldview of the West;
- *Animism* (which would include Hinduism, Buddhism, and eastern folk): the belief that the world is ultimately spiritual, in which the physical world is animated by spirits or gods;
- *Theism*: the belief in one personal, infinite God.

The Worldview Continuum[13]

Animism	Theism	Secularism
Ultimate Reality Is Spiritual	Ultimate Reality Is Personal	Ultimate Reality Is Physical

Every person and society can be found somewhere along a continuum, with secularism and animism at either end and with theism in the middle. So, how does a biblically informed view of history compare to the other worldviews?

---

[13] Figure from Darrow L. Miller, *Discipling the Nations: The Power of Truth to Transform Cultures* (Seattle: YWAM Publishing, 1998), 40.

A Biblical View of History

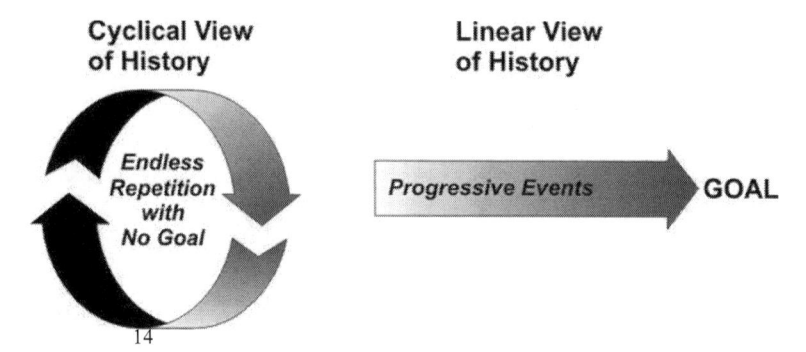

Cyclical View of History

Endless Repetition with No Goal

Linear View of History

Progressive Events → GOAL

The Christian worldview is linear. Indeed, most of the Western world has historically had a linear view based on the Judeo-Christian perspective. This does not mean that history never repeats itself. There are many examples where this has happened, largely because humankind often fails to learn from the mistakes of the past. For example, in seeking to conquer Europe, Hitler repeated Napoleon's mistake of invading Russia, which weakened his forces and significantly contributed to his defeat. However, overall, when stepping back to consider the "Big Picture," history has direction and is leading somewhere. It had a specific beginning (Creation) and will have a specific end (Day of Judgment). Regardless of how humans choose to influence history, God is ultimately directing human affairs toward an ultimate conclusion that centers around the lordship of Jesus Christ and bringing time and life on planet earth as we know it to an end, before the King returns with his kingdom and a new world order is ushered in to a recreated

---

[14] http://www.freesundayschoollessons.org/systematic-theology/lesson-22-the-place-of-the-church-in-history-biblical-foundations-for-living/.

earth, where everything will be as God originally intended.[15]

We have all been invited to join God in what he is doing across the earth, playing our unique part and contributing to the completion of a bigger plan. We should have a *progressive* view of a universal history as we see over time the unfolding plan of God.[16] Life has meaning and purpose.

This starts with the belief that history has an author, a Creator, and that humankind is the pinnacle of all creation, unique and made in the very image and likeness of God himself. This belief addresses a fundamental question common to all people throughout history: "Who am I, and what value does my life possess?"

For Christians who accept the Bible as the authoritative Word of God, the meaning of life and the meaning of history over time become clearer. We begin to understand other foundational concepts such as humanity's sin, the resulting separation from the life of God, God's grace and mercy in providing a Savior to restore and reconcile humanity back to himself through Jesus Christ. We could go on, but what is relevant is that as we look back through providential history, we can observe a progressive unfolding of God's heart and eternal purpose: a desire to reveal himself and have a relationship with his people, and through them to make himself known among all peoples of the earth, so that he can dwell in them and express his image through them throughout the earth.

---

[15] Revelation 21:4, 6; 22:3.
[16] Ephesians 1:11.

God Has a Dream

Many of us will be familiar with Martin Luther King's iconic "I Have a Dream" speech, in which Dr King called for racial equality and an end to racial discrimination. Decades later, this stirring speech continues to inspire other dreamers to live and fight for a whole range of different causes. However, did you know that God is also a dreamer? Since the beginning of time, God has dreamed of a world filled with people he can share his love with and who love him in return. It is a dream of a world filled with his truth, goodness and beauty, a world not corrupted by sin, without war, fear, pain, sickness, greed, poverty, and every other hostile thing. Instead, it is a place of peace, love, and unending joy. Such a world is what God is committed to recreating. God's dream is the coming of his kingdom on earth.

God's Mission Statement

In recent times the creation of mission statements has been in vogue. It seems every major business has one, many schools and other organizations have them, and numerous churches have also formulated their "mission" and have it on display to those coming through the doors of their church building or visiting their website. Have you ever given thought to the fact that God also has a mission statement and, if so, what it is and what it entails?

Just as it is vitally important for us to recognize that the whole of history throughout time is fundamentally a story of God's redemption of the whole of his creation, it is also vital that we understand that for this redemptive story to take place, God has his own mission to bring it to pass. What is exciting is to recognize that we have *all* been invited to be a part of *God with a mission!* It is in his mission that God invites us to join him and be a part of writing his story. This story has four key elements:

- *Creation*: in the beginning God
- *Rebellion/Fall*: man rebels against the High King of heaven and everything God made is infected by sin
- *Redemption*: the Cross to restore all that was lost (God's Mission)
- *Restoration/Consummation*: the return of the King!

As we grasp the fact that God is a missionary God who has sent himself through his Son, Jesus Christ, we will also understand the missionary calling as God's people. The church exists because of its mission and a church that is not "the church in mission" is no church at all.[17] This means that it is not that the church has a mission (perhaps expressed in a presentable mission statement) but that the mission of God has a church, which exists to be a sign and a witness to the nations, and a foretaste of God's dream for the world.

As we look at God's missionary plan revealed in the Old Testament, we see the choosing of Abram (later renamed Abraham), who became the father of all those who

---

[17] Lesslie Newbigin, *The Open Secret: An Introduction to the Theology of Mission* (Wm. B. Eerdmans Publishing, rev. ed. 1978, 1995), 2.

believe.[18] God tells Abram to leave his country and what was familiar to him with the promise that God would bless (empower and prosper) him in order that through him, all the families of the earth would also be blessed.[19] Here, we see right from the outset, God's mission was for *all peoples* of the earth. Not just for the purpose of isolated individual spirituality but for shared relationship with each other as "the families of the earth." Furthermore, it wasn't just concerned with people. It also related to a new land of promise, an unseen city designed and made by God himself.[20] The vision of a city that speaks of human relatedness and the commission to subdue the earth is a reference to God's kingdom which we will return to later on. This kingdom vision is the dream that motivates Abram to step out into the unknown.

Mission Agents

The method God would employ to achieve his mission would involve *selection* and *stewardship*. Those chosen were not selected for merely their own benefit but for the sake of those not chosen. The blessed were to be the bearers and stewards of the blessing for the all. They were blessed to be a blessing! How easy it can be for God's people to forget the second part of this covenant promise. We love the part about receiving the "top line" blessing of God but often fail to realize the reason for God's empowering: the "bottom line" responsibility to be a

---

[18] Romans 4:16.
[19] Genesis 12:1–3.
[20] See Hebrews 11:8–10.

blessing and empower others in all areas of life and society. We will return to this later.

Through Abraham, a nation was birthed, Israel, that was to be a witness to the true and living God for all other nations. Apart from some notable individual exceptions[21] Israel as a nation failed in its mandate to pass on the blessing which had been entrusted to her. Sadly, God's missionary nation lost sight of the responsibility it had been given of bringing a revelation of Israel's God being the one true God over all the earth.

In spite of this loss of understanding the mission of God, more significantly, all of human history—from the first man and woman to the Roman Empire—was working toward a moment in history that would change things forever. The Promised Messiah, not just for Israel but a Messiah for all peoples, Jesus of Nazareth, was to enter our world in a specific geographical location (Palestine) and at a precise moment which the Bible describes as "the fullness of time."[22]

God-Centered Drama

While human actions form the bulk of historical events, a biblical worldview sees God's acts to be at the center of its meaning. As stated before, history is really God's story and God (not man) is the primary "actor." We are also *all*

---

[21] For example, Joseph and Egyptians (Genesis 45:7–8); Moses and Pharaoh (Exodus 9:14–16); Joshua crossing Jordan River (Joshua 4:24); David and Goliath (1 Samuel 17:45–46); Daniel's interpretation of King Nebuchadnezzar's dream and fulfillment (Daniel 4:34–37); Daniel and King Darius (Daniel 6:26–27); Esther and Mordecai (Esther 8:8–17); Ruth and Naomi (Ruth 1:16); Old Testament prophets' warnings and prophecies.
[22] Galatians 4:4.

"actors" in God's story, who enter the stage at a particular point in time with the ability to create history and develop the earth,[23] being a channel of God's blessing to all nations. However, the key scene and pivotal moment and central focus of all history is the death and resurrection of God's Son, Jesus Christ. God had prophesied this event after humanity's fall, and everything had been progressing up to this point in time. Without it, history would fall to pieces, without a focus and without a purpose. The drama of history now comes into focus, the conflict of two kingdoms, between light and darkness, good and evil, God and Satan. It is not subjected to fate or chance, but all events have meaning as part of God's plan of the ages to sum up all things in Christ. From here on in, history will continue to be guided by a sovereign God, not in an endless cycle without a definite story ending, but toward the goal of Jesus Christ's triumphal return, the fullness of his kingdom, and him becoming all in all.

God's Mission Reaffirmed

Having completed the task given by the Father, Jesus commissions his own disciples with the words, "As the Father sent me, so I send you."[24] His mission is to be their mission. In his parting he leaves his followers with the familiar words we refer to as "the Great Commission."[25]

---

[23] The creation mandate for development is given in Genesis 1:28 and Genesis 2:15.
[24] John 20:21.
[25] Matthew 28:18–20, Mark 16:15.

"All authority has been given to me in heaven and on earth. Go therefore and make disciples of all the nations, baptizing them in the name of the Father and of the Son and of the Holy Spirit, teaching them to obey all that I have commanded you; and lo, I am with you always, even to the end of the age." (Matthew 28:18–20)

The truth is that this is not some new commission, some new assignment that Jesus gives as a last-minute afterthought before leaving to return to his Father. This is the same mission—God's mission—that was first given to Abram[26] and then to the nation of Israel. The Great Commission is therefore not really *given* at the end of the gospels, but *reaffirmed*.

So how do we view this Great Commission?

The Scope of God's Mission

A version of the Great Commission can be found in each of the synoptic gospels and in Luke's sequel, the Book of Acts.[27] Two thousand years have passed since Jesus gave his disciples his parting command recorded in Acts 1:8, "But you shall receive power when the Holy Spirit has come upon you; and you shall be witnesses to Me in Jerusalem, and in all Judea and Samaria, and to the end of the earth." A subtle change to this text has influenced the thinking of churches for hundreds of years, to the present day: the substitution of the word *then* for the word *and*.

---

[26] See Genesis 12:1-3.
[27] Matthew 28:18-20; Mark 16:15-18; Luke 24:47; John 20:21; Acts 1:8.

"You shall be witnesses to Me in Jerusalem, then in all Judea and Samaria, then to the end of the earth." Jesus did not use the word *then*; he used *and*. The change of one small word can radically alter our understanding and practice of mission.

Why is this subtlety so significant? Because a philosophy that adopts a "then" mentality gives us permission to think that Jerusalem is more important than Judea, Samaria, and the ends of the earth. "And" brings them together as equally important. "Then" allows us the luxury of forgetting those beyond our boundaries and comfort zones, while we focus on reaching those nearest and most similar to ourselves. "And" demands that we be aware of both. "Then" allows us to pass on responsibility to someone else. "And" empowers us to do both at the same time.

The key point of Jesus' commission is that, empowered by the Holy Spirit, we are to be witnesses to him in all four "areas," Jerusalem, Judea, Samaria, and the ends of the earth, at the same time. God does not give us the choice of home or abroad, our own people or those from another culture. He challenges us with the all-inclusive, all-embracing vision of home and abroad, our own culture and other cultures, bearing witness to him at the local level and to the ends of the earth simultaneously.

One philosophy often used to support the "then" mentality is that we should focus on and reach our "Jerusalem" first before attempting to go to those beyond our borders."[28] However, Jesus did not instruct his first disciples to wait around in Jerusalem until the people of that city had been reached before proceeding to the next group, akin to some kind of stage-by-stage business marketing strategy. This would be like a Christian who will only witness to his family and friends before being a witness for Christ to others. The task in Jerusalem will never be fully completed, and we will certainly never progress to the fourth and final "stage" of being a witness to the ends of the earth people if we wait until we have reached those closer to home. There will always be more to do "at home" that will keep us occupied and too busy to reach out to those further afield. If we as a church wait until we are "ready," until we have the resources, until "the time" is right, we may well find the time never comes.

Another reason given to support the "then" philosophy is that we shouldn't try and reach those beyond our immediate borders if we are not being successful in reaching those on our own doorsteps. This sounds right, but it is another way the enemy would seek to keep us contained within our own locality. A purpose of missions is to plant indigenous churches that are self-propagating, self-governing, and self-supporting. If we wait until we are functioning successfully at home before we reach out to those unreached with the gospel, the danger will be that we will seek to transplant what has been successful in our own church to a new setting where it doesn't fit and is culturally inappropriate. The truth is the gospel of Jesus Christ will work wherever; it is "the power of God to salvation for

---

[28] Jerusalem in the context of Acts 1:8 is generally interpreted to be our locality, although as Jesus' disciples were not from Jerusalem, it really equates to a strategic starting point.

everyone who believes."[29] Jesus never said to prove oneself as a witness at home before being a witness somewhere else. He said, wait until you receive the power of the Holy Spirit and then *"go!"* Sadly, for all the good things that were happening in the church at Jerusalem, it does not give us the right example to imitate in relation to the Great Commission, as for years they were reluctant to break out of familiar territory and only reached Jewish people like themselves.[30] As a result of their unwillingness to fully embrace the Great Commission, their influence waned.

In contrast, the church in Antioch *simultaneously* became a witness across cultural and geographical boundaries, becoming the first truly multicultural and multiethnic church (reflecting the cosmopolitan nature of the third largest city in the Roman Empire), and in so doing replaced the church in Jerusalem as the most significant church in the book of Acts. In addition, the church was prepared to release two key men into apostolic mission ministry.[31] Antioch therefore became a model of a sending church taking the gospel to the unreached and fulfilling the mandate of Acts 1:8.

God is always challenging us to extend our boundaries, enlarge our thinking, and expand our vision. However, there is more to God's mission than merely being broad in scope geographically, but before considering this further we need to deal with some thinking that can get in the way of truly understanding God's story.

---

[29] Romans 1:16.
[30] See Acts 11:19.
[31] Acts 13:1–3.

CHAPTER 2
FAULTY STORY PARADIGMS

Faulty Thinking

Throughout history there has been a clash of differing worldviews, and the church has had to contend for biblical truth. During the twentieth century, especially in the Western world, the attack has come from the proponents of secular humanism. Through a strategically planned and incremental approach using the educational system and other key shapers of culture such as arts and entertainment, and the media, this anti-God worldview has permeated all areas of the Western world, in an attempt to influence our thinking in subtle ways of which we are not always aware. It is only in looking back to how things were a few decades ago that one can see the huge changes that have occurred in the thinking of the general population and what is now considered "normal" and acceptable within society.

What is also shocking to discover is that sometimes our "Christian" beliefs and mindset, even our understanding of Scripture, can be influenced by the flawed thinking of previous generations or the prevailing culture of our day. For example, if you like me have grown up with an education based on a Western/Greek worldview, it focuses on the individual and a separation of the supernatural from the natural. This leads to thinking that as a Christian I am only responsible to God for living a godly life but not for being a steward of my nation, its laws, and society in general.

Our worldview is critical to how we see the Great Commission and our part in God's story. Many Christians have become disconnected from God's story and mission due to faulty thinking.

How Do We View *Mission* and *Missions*?

The terms "mission" or "missions" can mean different things to different people. Closely related is the English word "missionary," that is derived from Latin (the verb *"mitto,"* meaning "I send") and is the equivalent of the Greek-derived word "apostle" (*"apostolos"*), and means "sent one." Ask a number of Christians to define a missionary and you will receive a range of differing responses. Similarly, some will see a missionary as a distinct calling for certain believers, while today, increasing numbers of Christian leaders are referring to all believers as being missionaries! Given the potential for you to feel really confused, allow me to try and bring some clarity.

In the previous chapter we noted that God has a mission. Scholars refer to this in Latin as the *"missio Dei."* When we equate "mission" with the mission of God, then every believer is called to participate in and engage in what constitutes the total mission of the church. This is what this book is primarily about. "Missions," on the other hand, is a vital and distinctive task *within* the over-riding mission of God. It is therefore narrower than "mission" and relates to the intentional human activities that those called to be missionaries engage in to take the gospel to places where the gospel is not known. Having said that, missions isn't just another church activity that appeals to a select number of Christians. It isn't supposed to be one of the options offered on a church's menu of interest areas that a believer can sign up for. It is fundamentally deeper than that. God's mission must include "missions" because the mission of the Triune God extends to the ends of the earth. As we will see in a later chapter, missions is the ultimate horizon of the whole missionary task of the church and without it the church's involvement in the mission of God falls short and is incomplete. On an individual level, I believe every Christian should be involved in some way—through going, giving, or praying—as "missions" express the heart of God for all peoples and nations. That aside, God invites every believer to engage in his overall mission and to discover their lives in a story bigger than themselves. This means *you* have a place in God's mission! And yes, specially called and trained missionaries are not the only ones who go to the "mission field." You have a mission field too! Having a clear grasp of these terms is crucial to our understanding and involvement in the Great Commission.

The Need for a Biblical Worldview

As we have already noted, our worldview is critical to how we see reality. It shapes not only our understanding of life but also how we view God and interpret Scripture. When we come to Christ our minds have to be renewed from *our* way of seeing the world, which is essentially based on and inherited from our culture, to one that is in alignment with how *God* thinks.[32] Repentance is a changing of one's mind, but making Jesus Lord is only the initial step in the process. Having a kingdom worldview and the mind of Christ develops over a lifetime.

In Chapter 1 we noted that there are essentially three major worldviews: secularism, which assumes that reality is only physical; animism, which assumes that the universe is ultimately spiritual; and biblical theism, which believes in the God revealed in the Bible. What is shocking to realize is that many Christians do not hold to a biblical worldview. According to surveys carried out since 1995, only 19 percent of all American adults who professed to be "born-again Christians" had a biblical worldview.[33] So what is a biblical worldview?

What is a Biblical Worldview?

For the purposes of the above survey carried out by the Barna Group,[34] a "biblical worldview" was defined as believing that:

- absolute moral truth exists;
- the Bible is totally accurate in all of the principles it teaches;
- Satan is considered to be a real being or force, not merely symbolic;

---

[32] See Rom.12:2, 1 Cor. 2:16; 2 Cor. 10:4–5.
[33] http://www.barna.org/transformation-articles/252-barna-survey-examines-changes-in-worldview-among-christians-over-the-past-13-years.
[34] The Barna Group is a visionary research organization focused on the intersection of faith and culture (www.barna.org).

- a person cannot earn their way into Heaven by trying to be good or doing good works;
- Jesus Christ lived a sinless life on earth;
- God is the all-knowing, all-powerful creator of the world who still rules the universe today.

In the research, anyone who held all of those beliefs was said to have a "biblical worldview," although it is perhaps worth noting that the above "definition" equates more to an orthodox theology derived from a biblical worldview, rather than corresponding to a biblical worldview, which is far more encompassing than the six points listed in the Barna survey. As highlighted in Chapter 1, our worldview is like a lens through which we view everything in the world. To operate by a biblical worldview is to see *everything* through the Word of God and to "practice the Kingship of Jesus," living every area of our lives in obedience to and for the honor of Jesus Christ our Lord.[35]

Given the alarming statistic that the majority of American Christians (and it would not be unreasonable to assume that this would also apply to most Christians in the postmodern Western world as well) do not have a fundamental belief in the existence of moral truth, it is essential that there is a return to a belief in absolute truth based on God's Word, the Bible. Without doing so, on what basis can we present a case for social reform, for the discipling of our families, communities and nations, and for addressing the problems and evils in our world? If, as the

---

[35] http://www.colsoncenter.org/the-center/the-chuck-colson-center/what-is-biblical-worldview.

postmodernist would say, truth is relative and reality is only that which individuals or social groups make it to be, then we will soon be back to the time of the Judges when "everyone did what seemed right in their own eyes."[36] The good news that we have to offer must be grounded in the truth contained within God's manual for life, the Bible, for it is only in the truth that people and nations are set free.[37]

Indian philosopher Vishal Mangalwadi, in his landmark book, *Truth and Transformation: A Manifesto for Ailing Nations,* writes how the peculiar idea that the pursuit of knowledge is a divine calling came into Europe from the Bible via St. Augustine (AD 354–430). In teaching that God was a rational being and that the human mind (not just the human "soul" or "spirit") was made in God's image, Augustine believed that God had given us a mind like his own so that we might know him and understand and govern his creation as his children. Therefore, to be godly meant the cultivation of our minds, and as a result, unlike many other nations built on a nonbiblical worldview, "the Bible became the ladder on which the West climbed the heights of its educational, technical, economic, political, and scientific excellence." Mangalwadi then spells out the tragic results of discarding the moral secret of its success:

> Tragically, during the eighteenth and nineteenth centuries an intellectual movement known as the Enlightenment separated the West's confidence in reason from its biblical foundations. The end result was that the twentieth century intellectuals awoke to

---
[36] Judges 17:6; 21:25.
[37] John 8:32.

a realization that the West no longer had any foundations for its earlier confidence in human reason. Secular rationalism collapsed into skepticism, cynicism, mysticism, and the occult. Universities that were built to help students find truth and become servants of God and neighbors turned (at best) into factories producing workers for a technocratic age. Public education became incapable of training civilized citizens . . . Rational cynicism has now become the hallmark of secular universities . . . The West has exchanged its worldview shaped by the Bible for a lie that the human mind is an accident of blind chance, no more valid than an animal brain.[38]

As Elijah on Mount Carmel urged Israel to repent and return to her foundation—the truth—so must the body of Christ remain established on the bedrock of scripture and a biblical worldview.[39] This will challenge many of our paradigms and mindsets in terms of how we communicate God's story, the essential *metanarrative*,[40] and engage in God's mission. Some issues will be explored in this chapter. While this will be necessary in order to align our thinking with God's purposes, we must remain rooted in our biblical foundations and not be fashioned or tempted to conform to popular culture. When it comes to stories, these are now often viewed as 'myths'. In spite of the fact that

---

[38] Vishal Mangalwadi, *Truth and Transformation: A Manifesto for Ailing Nations* (Seattle: YWAM Publishing, 2009), 120.
[39] For more on this vital issue, I recommend Vishal Mangalwadi, *The Book That Made Your World: How the Bible Created the Soul of Western Civilization* (Nashville: Thomas Nelson, 2011).
[40] The one large story that all other stories fit into.

for many people there is no longer a belief in any overarching story about life which is true absolutely for all time and for all people, this doesn't change the reality that God's story is *truth*, the ultimate true story which transcends all peoples, cultures, and time. God's story is revealed through the Bible, which is the word of truth.[41]

Christian Influence in Society

Have you ever wondered why, if the Church worldwide is growing at such a tremendous rate (in Africa and Asia) and is now represented across the earth more than at any time in history,[42] the Christian faith is not having the influence that it should in the societies, cultures, and nations where it is in evidence? Certainly, most Christians would say that Christianity will have a positive influence on a community and that the more Christians there are in a nation, the greater the benefit to society at large. So, *why* are we not seeing more of the blessing, which should accompany the receiving of the gospel?

Take Africa for example. Africa is the most Christianized continent in the world and is estimated to be 80% Christian south of the Sahara.[43] There are hundreds and thousands of churches and evangelists. We would

---

[41] Psalm 119:160; John 14:6; 17:17
[42] Whilst it is difficult to give a definite answer to the actual number of Christians in the world, many sources mention 2.1 billion Christians in the world, which equates to about one third of the total population of the planet, (accessed 4 Oct 2010
http://wiki.answers.com/Q/How_many_Christians_are_there_worldwide).
[43] 82 percent according to the *Atlas of Global Christianity* edited by Todd M. Johnson and Kenneth R. Ross, Edinburgh University Press, 2009.

expect that, according to the Word of God, Africa would therefore be a blessed continent.

In Deuteronomy 28, we have God's perspective on what a blessed nation looks like and what a cursed nation looks like. Typically, nations today are judged by their average income levels, living standards and gross national product. However, the standard God uses is quite different. His profile of a blessed nation is like a national inventory covering a whole range of different areas of life such as family and relationships, work and economy, defense forces, the weather, and the national debt.

While nearly every person in the southern part of Africa has been "reached" with the gospel, the sad reality is that it has not really made a difference to the African nations where the gospel has been received.[44] With 30 of the 40 poorest countries in the world in Africa, there is widespread poverty, along with violence, disease, corruption, injustice, chaos and devastation. The African nation of Rwanda has experienced revival in recent decades but at the same time terrible poverty and civil war.[45] Uganda, which later became the center of this revival, has experienced two decades of terrible suffering with its economy being destroyed. There has been torture, murder, civil war and displacement of people, all of this having

---

[44] For further study refer to *Hope for Africa and What the Christian Can Do* by George Kinoti, published by the African Institute for Scientific Research and Development, 1994 (ISBN 9966–9922–0-0); and *Against All Hope: Hope for Africa* by Darrow L. Miller with Scott Allen and the African Working Group of Samaritan Strategy Africa
(http://www.disciplenations.org/uploads/ad/03/ad03adec9da6eeefd81156a14b0 03282/Against-All-Hope-Hope-for-Africa.pdf).

[45] The genocide in Rwanda in 1994 took place in a nation that claimed 84 percent of its ten million population then to be Christians.

taken place while the Ugandan Church was one of the strongest churches in Africa.

In an interview with Dr. Tokunboh Adeyemo, former General Secretary of the Association of Evangelicals in Africa and prior to his death, the Executive Director of the Centre for Biblical Transformation, John Brand, director of the African Inland Mission, asked the troubling question, "Why is it that the greatest prevalence of AIDS in Africa is often where there is the greatest Christian presence? And, why is it that many of the most evangelized countries are also the most corrupt?"[46]

While some people look at Africa and believe it has been cursed,[47] on the contrary, given its abundance of natural resources it can be considered the most blessed continent in the world. However, Africa's wealth and blessing remains largely untapped because the nation has not been sufficiently discipled in the ways of God.

Referring to what he calls "Africa's enigma," Dr. Adeyemo remarked, "I salute the early missionaries who came to us, but often the gospel did not get beyond skin deep because it did not transform our traditional worldview." In noting the fact that for decades evangelism and missionary activities in Africa have been directed at getting people saved and getting them to heaven, the Centre for Biblical Transformation cites cases of highly educated and well-trained clerics and leaders who indulge in such practices as divination, witchcraft, traditional religious

---

[46] The Blessing and the Enigma by John Brand (http://new.aimint.org/eu/explore/articles/94-the-blessing-and-the-enigma).
[47] The idea that Africa is cursed comes from an interpretation of Genesis 9:45 where Noah curses his son, Ham. Africans are said to descend from Ham and so therefore share in the curse. This interpretation was used by South African theologians as one of the justifications for Apartheid.

orgies, tribalism and spiritualism, not to mention social ills including immorality, violence and corruption.[48] Clearly, a superficial understanding of the gospel will not transform an unregenerate mind and will certainly not bring about the fundamental need of a redeemed, kingdom worldview necessary for societal transformation.[49]

Some people may be tempted to point out that while this has been the case, the important thing to remember is that the people in these nations have been blessed by receiving Jesus into their lives. It is true many have personally received the greatest gift available to humankind. However, this is where we as Christians, particularly those of us who would call ourselves "evangelical" Christians, have tended to overlook something critically important.

Diluted Worldview, Diluted Gospel

God has always wanted all of his children to engage in his mission and the "family business," but as we look back through history, for the most part, this has not occurred. The major reason for this non-participation has been a diluted worldview which has robbed many believers of the joy of knowing they had a unique contribution to make to the kingdom of God. This wrong thinking has also separated them from their mission, as part of God's mission, on the earth in their lifetime. As a consequence,

---

[48] The Centre for Biblical Transformation (www.designsbyore.com/cbt-web/index.html#)

[49] Whilst noting the lack of societal transformation within Africa, it is also sobering to acknowledge that in previously called "Christian" nations, shocking and unbelievable changes are taking place in western "post-Christian" societies that once professed Christianity but now reject their heritage.

those that participated tended to be those who were employed in some kind of "full-time" Christian work—missionaries, pastors, evangelists, Bible translators, etc.—leaving the majority of their fellow-believers on the sidelines. Some may have faithfully supported on the home front (through vital prayer and financial support) but most did not engage on the basis that they had not received any *special calling* from God to do so.

"No-one escapes the general call to mission. No-one can say, "Witness is not for me." The critical question is not whether we're called, for we are. The critical question is "Where am I called to?" The answer may be to serve Jesus right where we are already, among those we live with and work beside. That is a wholly legitimate calling."[50]

Before I quit my career and became a "missionary," I worked for a number of years in the UK electricity industry as a corporate administrator. On my last day at the office there was a staff gathering where management and staff thanked me for my service and wished me well for the future. I remember my senior manager's opening remarks clearly. He said, with a hint of emotion in his voice, "I am very disappointed that Stuart is leaving us but I believe he has found his vocation in life." Clearly, my manager recognized that since I was prepared to give up my career prospects and a good salary in order to pursue a new direction in my life that I really believed in, I had found my vocation, my purpose, my life's calling. The truth is, whether it requires a seemingly dramatic change in our lives or not, each of us has a unique vocation and purpose

---

[50] Alistair Brown, *I Believe in Mission* (Hodder and Stoughton, 1997), 104.

in life to discover, one that only we can fulfill and one that is of equal value in the sight of God.

The significance of each of our lives and our work is made clear in the words of the apostles Paul and Peter:

> "But to EACH ONE of us grace was given according to the measure of Christ's gift." (Ephesians 4:7, capitals mine)

> "As EACH ONE has received a gift, minister it to one another, as good stewards of the manifold grace of God." (1 Peter 4:10, capitals mine)

> "Now the body is not made up of one part but of many. If the foot should say, "Because I am not a hand, I do not belong to the body," it would not for that reason cease to be part of the body. And if the ear should say, "Because I am not an eye, I do not belong to the body," it would not for that reason cease to be part of the body. If the whole body were an eye, where would the sense of hearing be? If the whole body was an ear, where would the sense of smell be? But in fact God has arranged the parts in the body, EVERY ONE of them, just as he wanted them to be. If they were all one part, where would the body be? As it is, there are many parts, but one body." (1 Corinthians 12:14–20, capitals mine)

Darrow Miller, in stressing the vital need to reconnect our lives and work to God's mission, writes,

The roles that individual Christians play vary greatly, but each is critical to the larger effort of advancing God's kingdom. In fact, as Paul says, each person's role is specifically designed by God for that person and for the sake of the body. No person, no work that is ethical, is holier, more blessed, more godly, more essential than any other. Every Christian, not just the Christian pastor or leader or missionary, must begin to recognize the significance of his or her own life and work, which God has designed to be an integral part of the body and without which the body is incomplete. Our work, your work, is part of God's mission on earth, and this includes not simply your "career"—although that is an important part of it—but all arenas of life, every occupation and activity you undertake."[51]

While the Bible expounds a wholistic[52] worldview that does not divide the spiritual and natural realms, and maintains a unified understanding of life and relationship with God, influences from other worldviews and philosophies have influenced the thinking of Christians during different periods of history.[53] Greek philosophers such as Plato and Pythagoras introduced schools of thought

---

[51] Darrow L. Miller, *LifeWork: A Biblical Theology for What You Do Every Day* (Seattle: YWAM Publishing, 2009), xxiii.

[52] In the context of Christian ministry, the word "wholistic/holistic" refers to ministry that applies the whole Gospel to the whole person. The former spelling is used to be consistent with the idea of wholeness (the whole Gospel, the whole world, the whole person).

[53] For a detailed account see chapter 2 of Darrow Miller's excellent book *LifeWork*, entitled "How Did We Get Here? Dualism throughout Church History."

that lessened the value of the physical world. This was strengthened by the Eastern worldview, found today in Hinduism and Buddhism, which emphasizes the reality of the spiritual realm while discounting the physical as a mere illusion of reality. In time such dualistic patterns of thought impacted on mainstream Christianity as seen in the development of monasticism where there were two levels of Christian life. The superior religious class consisted of religious workers such as monks, priests, nuns, and theologians. Everyone else was seen as belonging to the common and spiritually inferior class. Does this sound familiar even today where we have divisions between the clergy and the laity, those in "full-time" Christian work and those who have "secular" professions?

Although the Protestant Reformation challenged this dualistic worldview that had crept into the church during the Middle Ages and stressed that all work, provided it was not evil but consecrated before God, was sacred and of equal value, the Pietist movement in the seventeenth century brought a focus once again on the spiritual realm and the need for Christians to separate themselves from the world.

In the early eighteenth century, the Great Awakening that swept both England and the American colonies once again brought an emphasis on a personal faith that also led to active involvement in society and the culture at large. God was viewed as sovereign over all of life and not just the spiritual realm. By participating in the Great Awakening's recovery of a wholistic biblical worldview, evangelicals rejoined God's work in the world, transforming the British Empire and founding the United

States of America, perhaps the most free, just, and economically prosperous nation in human history.[54]

This dynamic for societal transformation was relatively short-lived as the nineteenth century brought the onslaught of secular materialism, ushering in a modern era built on the absolute denial of the spiritual realm. Work was therefore of no significance other than for the material rewards that it provided. Only the secular and material were recognized, given the belief that the spiritual was imaginary and did not exist. As a response to this challenge, the church denied the significance of the secular and elevated the spiritual, once again adopting the ancient Greek sacred-secular dualistic worldview. In terms of engaging with God's mission, the Great Commission was carried out by those who responded to the higher, religious calling of "full-time Christian service." Christians who became pastors, missionaries or evangelists were doing "spiritual" work, while the rest of the Christian "workforce" divided their lives into spiritual on Sundays and secular during the rest of the week.

Evangelicalism's Spiritual and Secular Divide

Drawing from the ancient Greek dichotomy there has been a division in Christian thinking between what is considered "spiritual," eternal and what *really* matters, from that which is merely "secular," temporary and material.[55] This issue became particularly pronounced at the beginning of the

---

[54] Miller, 27.
[55] The spiritual world is the realm of church, Bible study and prayer meetings, while the secular world is everything else. Such dualism is also referred to as Gnosticism, and in the context of Christianity, Evangelical Gnosticism.

twentieth century when the wholistic concept of the Hebrew word "shalom" (meaning peace, prosperity, welfare, well being, wholeness, harmony, nothing missing and nothing broken), was reduced to an overemphasis on the spiritual salvation of the individual. This period became referred to as "The Great Reversal" and led to Christians siding with one of two extremes of theological thought, namely evangelism or social concern. One side focused on social reform and thought corporate change would result in the change of individuals. The other side believed that if individuals experienced personal redemption, society as a whole would eventually change.[56]

Humanitarian help by itself will not change the hearts of people and society at large. Gospel for Asia founder, K. P. Yohannan, writes,

> In few countries is the failure of Christian humanism more apparent than in Thailand. There, after 150 years of showing marvelous social compassion, the Church still makes up only one-tenth of one percent of the entire population.
>
> Self-sacrificing missionaries probably have done more to modernize the country than any other single force. They gave the country the core of its civil service, education and medical systems. Working closely with the royal family, the missionaries played a crucial role in eliminating slavery and

---

[56] Debra Buenting's article, "Youth With A Mission and the Great Reversal," included in Part 3 of the book *His Kingdom Come: An Integrated Approach to Discipling the Nations and Fulfilling the Great Commission* (Seattle: YWAM Publishing, 2008), 150.

keeping the country free of Western control during the colonial era.

Thailand owes to missionaries its widespread literacy, first printing press, first university, first hospital, first doctor and almost every other benefit of education and science. In every area, including trade and diplomacy, Christian missionaries put the needs of the host nation first and helped usher in the twentieth century.

But today virtually all that remains of this is a shell of good works. Millions have meanwhile slipped into eternity without the Lord. They died more educated, better governed and healthier—but they died without Christ and are bound for hell.[57]

Similarly, evangelism and personal redemption will not automatically result in kingdom transformation within society. While some have argued the case for or against a "social" gospel, oftentimes churches and missionaries have preached an incomplete message that has left those reached with a segregated view of life.

A British journalist produced a television documentary to investigate the claim that a Christian presence in a community will bring about a positive impact and is a good influence. Taking regular church attendance as the indicator of a community being "Christianized," the journalist chose to look at the social demographics of the

---

[57] K. P. Yohannan, *Revolution in World Missions* (Gospel for Asia Books, 1986), 110.

city of Dallas, Texas, which at the time had more people per capita in church than any other community in the country. Life in Dallas was examined by considering various statistics and studies across a range of areas including crime, public safety, police enforcement, health care, hospitals, contagious diseases, infant mortality rate, education, jobs and employment, the economy, housing, homelessness, and racism. All of these categories were then compared with other cities which had significantly less people attending church on a regular basis. The study concluded that Dallas was one of the worst cities to live in—the crime, the decrepit social systems, the disease, the economic discrepancies, the racial injustice all disqualified this community from having an adequate quality of life. The journalist then spoke with respected leaders of the churches within the city. In asking for a response to his findings about the condition of their city and community, the answer was essentially the same: "This is not my concern . . . I'm a spiritual leader."[58]

Hopefully these findings should shock us. However, they are not unique to Dallas. It is a sad fact to accept that the non-Christian journalist's findings would be typical of most communities throughout the world even where there is a high presence of Christians. The tendency for the Church is to focus on what happens within the walls of the church building with its various programs and activities throughout the year. Evangelistic efforts, where they exist, follow an *"attractional"* model, based around getting people to come to church rather than the church going to

---

[58] Landa L. Cope, *An Introduction to The Old Testament Template* (The Template Institute Press, 2006), chapter 1.

represent the kingdom of God by being among the people (an *"incarnational"* approach) and equipping its members to do "kingdom work" from Monday to Saturday. Jesus showed us the way by coming to earth and living among humanity.

CHAPTER 3
THE BIG STORY OF GOD'S KINGDOM

Losing the Plot

Have you ever got so focused on the fine details that you lost the big picture of what was going on? Some people are more like that. They like to focus on the small details, dotting every 'i' and ensuring every 't' is crossed. We would be in big trouble without such detail-oriented people. However, if we only focus on the details we are in danger of missing the big picture and what is really important. This can happen when we read the Bible. While it is necessary to study the individual books and themes contained within Scripture, we must remain mindful of the overall story and purpose.

> "You have your heads in your Bibles constantly because you think you'll find eternal life there. But you miss the forest for the trees. These Scriptures are all about me! And here I am, standing right before you, and you aren't willing to receive from me the life you say you want." (John 5:39–40, The Message)

Story gives context. The Bible is a story which shapes history and gives meaning to our lives. Unfortunately, we can sometimes focus so much on the finer details that we lose the plot or view things out of context. We miss the big picture and main storyline of what God is doing. On this subject, Todd Hunter writes,

> For hundreds of years people studying the Bible have done so in fragmented ways. We've broken the text into its smallest parts—often individual words or portions of them—for analysis. Then we place them back into their sentence, paragraph, book, Testament, and finally the whole Bible. It sounds reasonable, doesn't it? I'm not sure what went wrong here, but something did. In most cases the *story* was lost in the process. The smallest bits, when added up, never quite became a narrative again. In other cases the reassembled bits told a different, truncated story.[59]

This is also applicable when it comes to the gospel. Are we missing the bigger picture of what the gospel is really about? Is our gospel too narrow?

The Gospel of the Kingdom

What gospel are we proclaiming? In seeking an answer to this question we need to be willing to ask some tough questions. We need to examine and reevaluate our worldview which will shape everything we do including the gospel that we seek to impart to others. For instance, if you were asked to explain the gospel, what would you say? If

---

[59] Todd D. Hunter, *Christianity Beyond Belief: Following Jesus for the Sake of Others* (InterVarsity Press, 2009), 39–40.

you are an evangelical Christian, I am sure you would highlight the key truths of man's sinfulness, the need for a Savior, and God's provision of his Son, Jesus Christ, who through his death on the cross and resurrection paid the price of sin and makes it possible for humankind to have a personal relationship with God and the gift of eternal life through repentance and faith in him.[60] While these truths are the essential components concerning salvation, they constitute only a part of the gospel that Jesus proclaimed.

In the gospel accounts Jesus emphasized the kingdom of God.[61] It was his inaugural message[62], a recurring theme in his teachings, and his focus during the forty days between the resurrection and his ascension back to his Father.[63]

> "And Jesus went about all Galilee, teaching in their synagogues, preaching the *gospel of the kingdom*, and healing all kinds of sickness and all kinds of disease among the people."[64]

> "Then Jesus went about all the cities and villages, teaching in their synagogues, preaching the *gospel of the kingdom*, and healing every sickness and every disease among the people."[65]

---

[60] The Christian message of salvation has been popularized by The Four Spiritual Laws, which were developed to help Christians explain the fundamentals of the Christian faith concerning salvation.
[61] Jesus mentioned "church" twice (Matthew 16:18 and 18:17), compared to over one hundred references to "the kingdom".
[62] see Mathew 4:17, 23; Mark 1:14–15; Luke 4:43.
[63] Acts 1:3.
[64] Matthew 4:23.
[65] Matthew 9:35.

"But He said to them, "I must preach the *kingdom of God* to the other cities also, because for this purpose I have been sent."[66]

Jesus made it clear that he would not return until the *gospel of the kingdom* had been preached as a witness to all nations.[67] He also taught his disciples to seek first the kingdom of God and his righteousness,[68] and to pray that his Father's kingdom—God's rule and way of doing things—come and for his will to be done on earth as it is in heaven.[69] This was no mere form of liturgy but an invitation to cooperate in seeing God's dream for his world come to pass. God's dream for the world is about the redemption of all creation, not just the saving of humankind and individuals getting into heaven; it is about the restoration of life as God intended it to be; it is about realigning life around God and God's ways.[70]

" . . . that in the dispensation of the fullness of the times He might gather together in one all things in Christ, both which are in heaven and which are on earth–in Him." (Ephesians 1:10)

The gospel that Jesus preached was the gospel of the kingdom, which is far more en-compassing than the saving of the individual soul, as wonderful and vitally

---

[66] Luke 4:43.
[67] Matthew 24:14.
[68] Matthew 6:33.
[69] Matthew 6:10.
[70] Alan J. Roxburgh and M. Scott Boren, *Introducing The Missional Church: What It Is, Why It Matters, How to Become One* (Baker Books, 2009), 101–102.

important as this is. Even on an individual level it isn't just about altar calls or commitments to Christ, people "getting a ticket to heaven," but making Jesus Lord and living according to God's ways. Furthermore, while the gospel of the kingdom will begin in the transforming of individual lives, it will also extend outwards to impact families and neighborhoods, communities and nations, manifesting God's will on earth "as it is in heaven." Without this, the gospel—the "good news"—will remain solely at an individual level instead of teaching nations God's way of doing things and little reformation will take place because the gospel of the kingdom has not been presented.

T. M. Moore writes:

> The gospel of the kingdom has become captive to mere personal interest, felt needs, aspirations of prosperity, postmodern relativism, and social and political ambitions. Certainly there are aspects of these in the gospel of the kingdom; however, the gospel of the kingdom is much broader, much deeper, much more integrated, and much more sweeping in its implications and power than any or all of its present-day substitutes. What we need today is a movement to restore the gospel of the kingdom—Christianity as a worldview—to the churches and the public square. This will not happen without the deliberate, coordinated effort of those who share a burden for such a broad and deep renewal.[71]

---

[71] T. M. Moore, "From Worldview Programs to Kingdom Movements," in *Truth and Transformation*, 265.

If every believer is going to engage in the Great Commission, it is imperative that they understand the nature of God's kingdom and the scope of God's work in the world. In spite of three years of walking with Jesus, his disciples still did not grasp what the kingdom was, its scope, and how it was to be revealed on the earth, let alone their role in bringing God's reign to the world. In fact, they thought there was little more to do than to wait for it, believing that Jesus was about to establish it himself. Many Christians today share the same misunderstanding, believing that now that they are saved, all they need to do is wait for Jesus to return the second time and take them to heaven. Such a mindset leads to a passive acceptance of the ills within society and the world, allied with the dualistic thinking (referred to in the previous chapter) that keeps their faith private and ineffective, as if it has nothing to offer this world and no power or relevance in the present.[72]

When we consider the engagement with the Great Commission over the years by missionaries and evangelical Christians in general, there has been an emphasis on the sharing of the gospel message and starting churches, but in some cases with neglect of the vital task of discipleship, especially with a view to the discipling of nations.[73] Here it is not so much neglect in expounding the theological truths from Scripture, but in the training and modeling of the practical areas of living life such as how to raise a family, handle money, run a business, extend God's kingdom in the workplace, or build and govern a righteous nation. It is a

---

[72] See Miller, *LifeWork*, 51.
[73] Matthew 28:19.

result of a gospel that limits itself to the preaching of salvation and how to function "spiritually."

Clearly, the gospel message must include salvation, but it must not be the only goal. Jesus never referred to the "gospel of salvation" but taught the "gospel of the kingdom." This is what will bring about transformation, not just to the lives of individuals but also to their families, neighborhoods, communities, and eventually to nations. True revival may start with the individual but will lead to a significant reformation and redemption on a broader scale through a revived church's influence on society at large.

CHAPTER 4

THE TRANSFORMING STORY OF GOD'S KINGDOM

Does a vision for the kingdom of God drive the church today? The sad reality is that much of the church has lost the biblical vision of the kingdom of God. She is largely divided into two groups, each with a very different understanding of the kingdom of God. The first understands the kingdom of God as somewhat intangible, invisible, mystical, heavenly, and in the future. These Christians state that Jesus is Lord of all but his kingdom will affect things here on earth only when Jesus returns at the end of history. The second group, in contrast, understands that the kingdom of God is to make a difference here and now.

Landa Cope, founder of The Template Institute,[74] writes,

> The first church transformed Israel, revolutionized the Roman Empire, and laid foundations for Western European countries to become the most prosperous nations in the world. What a different impact we see in modern mission history. Evangelized Africa is worse today in every arena—disease, crime, justice, economics, and the family—than before Christianity came to the continent.

---

[74] The Template Institute at the University of the Nations, www.templateinstitute.com.

America has a huge and apparently increasing percentage of practicing believers and, yet, it also is decreasing in moral fiber and quality of life in every category. Missionary workers in the sub-continent of India say that, while we quote that Nagaland is eighty percent Christianized, we fail to note that seventy percent of the teenagers in the capital city are drug addicts. Rwanda, with some sixty years of on-going revival in the church, suffers genocide in tribal civil war. Some say that there are more Christians alive today than the sum total of Christians in history. Where is the power to influence and transform communities that the Apostle Paul, St. Patrick, Calvin and many others experienced in their day?[75]

A Comprehensive Vision of the Kingdom of God!

If we are to have a compelling vision of the kingdom of God where his will and intentions are carried out on earth as they are in heaven, it also needs to be a *comprehensive* vision. We are all too aware of the far-reaching and devastating consequences that resulted from the rebellion of Adam and Eve in the Garden of Eden. The resultant comprehensive brokenness has plagued humanity ever since—wars, hatred, violence, environmental destruction, injustice, corruption, idolatry, poverty and famine. In response, God's redemptive plan to redeem his creation

---

[75] Landa L. Cope, *An Introduction to the Old Testament Template* (The Template Institute Press, 2006), 21-22.

from the effects of sin could not be narrow but included *everything* broken through the Fall.

Why did Jesus die on the cross? Was it to save us from sin and purchase our salvation? Yes, this was certainly a key part of it but it was not the sole purpose. God's agenda was much BIGGER than that! Colossians 1:19–20 says that Jesus came "to reconcile (restore, redeem) to himself all things, whether things on earth or things in heaven, by making peace through his blood, shed on the cross." It was a cosmic plan, a worldwide restoration project! This is what the coming of God's kingdom to earth represents—a total, global transformation in which everything is impacted, not just the lost souls of humanity. God's kingdom, which was foreshadowed in the Old Testament arrived with Jesus Christ. Jesus was the kingdom of God personified—he was the express image, nature and will of God.[76] He brought the substance of the kingdom to earth although in its fullest sense it is still to come. The first advent of Jesus made the kingdom of God a present reality; his second coming will result in the kingdom being fully realized. Our task as the church in this "in-between time," is to extend the blessings of God's kingdom throughout creation.

So what does this mean for us as his kingdom agents in the earth?

The Missing Component of the Great Commission

Referring back to the comments on worldview in Chapter 1, this is an area where many Christians are limited by

---

[76] Hebrews 1:3.

individualistic thinking and do not engage their minds on a macro level whereby they have a role in extending the kingdom of God in a community or nation. The truth is, on the whole (as there are always exceptions) the gospel that has been preached has mainly been a personal matter and has majored on getting people saved and starting churches. As wonderful as this is, it is not enough as it only addresses *one part* of the Great Commission mandate. Preaching the gospel to every person (Mark 16:15) is just *the beginning*. God's perspective is much bigger than just seeing people "saved." His heart has always been for nations.[77]

> "Ask of Me and I will give you the NATIONS for your inheritance, the ends of the earth for your possession." (Psalm 2:8, capitals mine)

The second and often overlooked part of the Great Commission mandate is recorded in Matthew 28: 19–20.

> "Go therefore and make DISCIPLES OF ALL THE NATIONS, baptizing them in the name of the Father and of the Son and of the Holy Spirit, teaching them to obey all that I have commanded you . . ." (capitals mine)

The King James Version of the Bible translates verse 19 as, *"teach all nations."* Young's Literal

---

[77] The word *"nations"* is recorded over two thousand times in Scripture. The Greek word is *'ethne'* from which we get our word 'ethnic' and refers to ethnic or cultural people groups. However, in Genesis 10 'nation' is defined as (a) people, (b) [ownership of] territory or land, and (c) language. It is therefore land and governance that also makes nations which is why God promised these to Abraham and not just descendants.

translation reads, *"disciple all the nations."* Whereas Mark's account focuses on preaching and on every single individual, Matthew uses a different verb—disciple—and focuses not on the individual or personal level, but on the corporate and national level. This vital part of Jesus' mandate relates to discipleship which is the process of leading a person to transformation according to the Bible. However, while the process begins with individuals, the command specifically relates to discipling entire nations. When Jesus commissioned his disciples he was asking them to fulfill God's promise made to Abraham in Genesis 12 that he would make him a 'great nation' and through his seed make all the nations great.

God's concern for both the individual and corporate expressions of humanity can be found throughout the Old Testament. We see God's care for individuals such as Abraham, David, Ruth, and Esther. God chose the nation of Israel in order to show himself to all the other nations. Sometimes the prophets of old directed their words to individuals. At other times they spoke a message to cities or nations.

In the New Testament we see Jesus ministering to individuals but he also had a passion towards peoples and nations. Reaching out to one woman resulted in many Samaritans acknowledging him as the Savior of the world. Prophetically seeing the destruction of Jerusalem caused him to weep for the nation of Israel. And as we have seen, he commanded all followers to disciple all nations.

What this all means is that instead of having a narrow and limited view of the gospel, focused solely on the saving of souls and personal morality, we understand that the gospel of the kingdom brings substantial healing to every aspect of our lives and every part of creation. It means we recognize the scope of the Great Commission is not limited solely to an individual or personal level, but also relates to the discipling and teaching of whole nations what God's will and intentions are in every sphere of society—in business, in education, in media, in the family, in arts & entertainment, in government, and so on—permeating cultures with the teachings of the kingdom of God until a society's worldview is transformed. To this task God calls every believer to be a part and engage in his kingdom mission. In fact, Jesus was the first person to ever connect the verb "to disciple" with the direct object "nations" in one sentence. So how is this discipling of nations to be carried out?

The "How to" of Nation Discipling

Matthew records four key verbs but in the Greek only one is a commandment: "disciple." The other three verbs describe how the discipling is to be carried out, by "going . . . baptizing . . . and teaching."

GO!
As disciples of Jesus we are to go to the nations like Jesus did, leaving our comfort zones and becoming mobile, identifying with the people with compassion and servant hearts, while also bringing the truth of God's kingdom to bring godly transformation to all areas of society that have been marred by humankind's fall.

IMMERSE!

We are also to "baptize" the nations. How is this to be done? We normally think of water when we hear the word "baptize." However, out of the fifteen times the gospels record Jesus using the verb "to baptize," only three times relate to water baptism. Nine references are in relation to suffering and his sacrificial death, while the other two times relate to Holy Spirit baptism. Within the context of the Great Commission passage, one way is to see the reference to baptize in terms of the individual public expression of repentance and faith through water baptism. Remembering that the root meaning of "baptize" is to immerse, another possibility is that Jesus is telling us to immerse and saturate the nations in the name—in an understanding of the character and ways—of God.

TEACH!

This naturally leads us onto the third "how to," teaching them to obey everything that Jesus commanded. This goes beyond mere head knowledge. We are told to permeate cultures with the teachings of the kingdom of God until a society's worldview is transformed.[78] The redemption of a culture doesn't mean its destruction or the loss of that culture's uniqueness. Rather, it will bring out the best contribution a nation can offer to its own people and to the rest of the world.

---

[78] For a fuller description of these "how to's," including an explanation of the four key verbs in the original Greek language, see David J. Hamilton's article, The New Testament Basis for Discipling Nations, included in *His Kingdom Come: An Integrated Approach to Discipling the Nations and Fufilling the Great Commission* (Seattle: YWAM Publishing, 2008).

As we read in Psalm 2:8, God the Father has given the nations of the earth to his Son, Jesus. They belong to him. As the Church worldwide, Jesus gave us the authority and responsibility to disciple and teach the nations for him. No nation, people, society or culture is to be excluded. Sadly, for the most part, we have failed and by default have allowed the evil one to have too much influence. Not only is it a fact that nearly 30% of the world's population have never even heard the gospel, in the West, the Judeo-Christian foundations that formed the basis for much of the development and moral fabric of society are now under attack from other atheistic and humanistic worldviews.

Pioneered by the so-called "Father of Modern American Education," John Dewey, secular humanists have pursued a specific agenda to turn people away from a belief in a Creator God and the teachings of the Bible, to the extent that in many Western nations today, Christians are marginalized in society and positively discriminated against. Whereas before, the Church had a voice in society, it has now lost the high ground and its right to speak.

Religious freedom within Europe was a hard-won achievement but today this is at risk as we are witnessing a gradual erosion of freedom of expression and conscience. Instances of intolerance and discrimination include the rejection of Christian candidates because of their faith, the sacking of someone because she wears a cross around her neck, or Christian hoteliers being persecuted for refusing to take in homosexual guests—as has happened in England. A recent legal case in the UK involved a Christian couple who lost their battle in the High Court over the right to become foster carers because they were not willing to tell a small child that the practice of homosexuality was a good thing. This landmark ruling leaves a precedent that Christian values will no longer be protected by English law.[79] Andrea Minichiello-Williams, director of Christian Concern,[80] warns of the eventual criminalization of Christianity in public:

> There's been a massive move by the secularist lobby to privatize religion. You can have faith so long as it doesn't affect you in the workplace. So long as you don't bring it into the workplace. Just make it private. It can't be public. It can't affect what you do in the public square.[81]

So how is the Church to respond in the face of such anti-Christian prejudice and persecution? In the coming years this will increasingly be an issue for Christians to respond to, wherever they are living. One thing is clear, rather than retreat back into our churches to find solace with other like-minded people, we must be willing to speak up for truth, justice and freedom. We must not disengage and become isolated within society, confirming their reasoning that the Church has lost its relevance to life in the twenty-first century. Whether it is popular or not, while not being self-righteous or judgmental, we must continue to seed our communities and nations with the life of the kingdom of God, and demonstrate the life-transforming

---

[79] http://www.bbc.co.uk/news/uk-england-derbyshire-12598896 (accessed 11 May 2011).
[80] http://www.christianconcern.com.
[81] http://www.cbn.com/cbnnews/world/2009/July/Britains-War-on-Christianity-Americas-Future-Fight/ (accessed 11 May 2011).

power of Jesus Christ. Jesus said, "All authority in heaven and earth has been given to me"[82] and it is with this authority the Church is to participate in the building of his kingdom through our lives and work, taking the kingdoms of this world from under the power of the evil one, and bringing every domain and sphere of life under the lordship of Christ.[83]

Engaging with the Spheres of Society

Spheres of Society

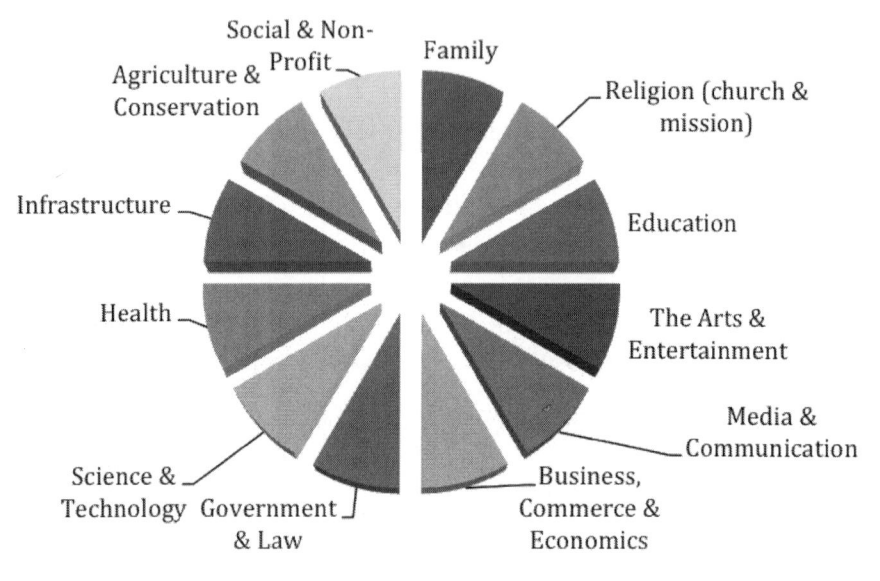

- Social & Non-Profit
- Family
- Agriculture & Conservation
- Religion (church & mission)
- Infrastructure
- Education
- Health
- The Arts & Entertainment
- Science & Technology
- Media & Communication
- Government & Law
- Business, Commerce & Economics

In 1975, Loren Cunningham and Bill Bright, founders of Youth With A Mission and Campus Crusade for Christ respectively, both received independently from God the

---

[82] Matthew 28:18.
[83] Hebrews 10:13.

same list of seven influential areas of society that Christians should intentionally engage with. The Christian writer and philosopher, Dr. Francis Schaeffer,[84] had also received the same message. I have expanded the original list of seven spheres to be discipled in the above diagram and as follows (not in any particular order):[85]

- Family
- Religion (church and mission)
- Government and Law
- Education
- The Arts, Entertainment and Recreation (celebration)
- Media and Communication
- Business, Commerce and Economics
- Science and Technology
- Infrastructure[86]
- Health
- Agriculture and Conservation
- Social and Non-Profit

The reference to *spheres* comes from 2 Corinthians 10:13 where the apostle Paul writes about the sphere he had been called to. Instead of the term *spheres* or *domains* of society, some Christians refer to *the gates* of the city or

---

[84] Along with his wife, Edith, Francis Schaeffer began L'Abri (French for "the Shelter") Fellowship in Switzerland in 1955.
[85] List of spheres and domains based on work of the Disciple Nations Alliance (see www.MondayChurch.org).
[86] The basic facilities, services, and installations needed for the functioning of a community or society, such as transportation and communications systems, water and power lines, and public institutions including schools, post offices, and prisons (www.thefreedictionary.com).

mountains of culture, which will one day come under the chief mountain representing God's kingdom rule. Scriptures referring to the kingdom of God as a mountain include Daniel's interpretation of Nebuchadnezzar's vision where the stone that struck the image became a great mountain and filled the whole earth[87], and the prophecies recorded in Isaiah 2:2 and Micah 4:1–2 where we read:

> "Now it shall come to pass in the latter days that the mountain of the LORD's house shall be established on the top of the mountains, and shall be exalted above the hills; and people shall flow to it. Many nations shall come and say, "Come, and let us go up to the mountain of the LORD, to the house of the God of Jacob; He will teach us His ways, and we shall walk in His paths."

The metaphorical concept of "the gates of the city" can be traced to the very real-world importance of these structures in biblical times. The gates of the city played a critical social and civic function in the ancient world and were the place where all kinds of public life and discourse took place, as well as providing for the defense of a city.[88]

Darrow Miller writes,

> Today, our societies are languishing because the metaphorical gates of our cities have largely been abandoned by the very people who can bring the person of Christ and the transforming power of the

---

[87] Daniel 2:35.
[88] Miller, *LifeWork*, chapter 18, The Gates of the City.

gospel into the lifeblood of society. God wants the descendants of Abraham to occupy the gates of the cities for the purpose of blessing the nations. When we combine this calling with being Christians who have a gospel that saves, redeems, renews, and restores, and with the worldview of Scripture, which instructs us about working out its transforming vision for the world through our callings in every area of life, then we get a glimpse of the potential. Vision like this has brought unprecedented economic development, political freedom, the rule of law, and the concept of universal education into much of the world. It has brought the emancipation of slaves and dignity to women. In other words, it has given humankind its humanity. Christian stewardship of "the gates," therefore, is vital for the life of our societies. Whoever takes responsibility for the gates will set the agenda for the health or destruction of society.[89]

While not needing to be limited to the spheres or domains listed above, they provide a useful framework for recognizing the key areas of any society. Furthermore, each of the spheres will contain thousands of sub-groups. Wherever God has called us to work, *everything* can be done for the glory of God. All kinds of work can be sanctified and "holy" unto the Lord, not just what takes place in the pulpit on a Sunday or within the context of "church" work, or "full-time" Christian service. Everyone from businesspeople, educators, actors, entertainers, artists

---

[89] Miller, *LifeWork*, 212.

and sportsmen and women to husbands, wives and parents, politicians, writers, lawyers and scientists has a vital and unique contribution to make within their particular spheres of life and society in discipling the nations in the ways of God . . . everyone has a God-given place in fulfilling the Great Commission! Part 3 of this book is designed to help you in discovering the unique role that God has designed you for.

Case Studies

This all sounds good in theory but how will it come about in practice? Simply put, the Word of God must be applied in each of the spheres and in every area of life. This doesn't mean there is a simple model that just needs to be used in every culture and society. Life is more complex than applying a "one-size-fits-all" model. It will require a dependency on the Holy Spirit to know how to apply biblical truth and the principles God has given to guide us.

While I believe God is now reawakening his Church to her responsibility to disciple nations through the spheres or "mountains" of society and culture, as we look back in history we will discover that different men and women of God have been engaged in these same areas of society for hundreds of years. The Christian church has a long history of involvement in all aspects of life including government, education, healthcare, the arts, and social action. Catholic monks carried their missionary message throughout Europe, encouraging converts to develop every aspect of their lives, from private devotion to academic scholarship.[90] Monasteries became centers of faith, learning, and technical progress. Pietists, Moravians, Methodists, and Puritans fed and clothed the poor, established schools, and fought for social issues such as the rights of women and slaves. The Reformers, too, were concerned with foundational social issues.[91] Let's look at some case studies.

Nation of Israel
In the Old Testament we do find an example where we see God discipling, through Moses, the nation of Israel (studying the book of Deuteronomy from the perspective of the various spheres of influence in a society—government, economics, science and technology, healthcare, family, etc.—is a good place to start).[92] In about 300 years God took some three million refugees and turned them into a kingdom whose reputation and fame travelled far and wide so that another head of state, the Queen of Sheba, wanted to learn about its wisdom and education, just laws and prosperity.[93] After turning away from God's ways the kingdom was divided and experienced decline. The young King Josiah was a biblical reformer who, at the age of 26, rediscovered the Law of Moses (particularly the book of

---

[90] Ronald J. Sider, ed., *Evangelicals and Development: Towards a Theology of Social Change* (Philadelphia: Westminster Press, 1981).
[91] Debra Buenting's article, Youth With A Mission and the Great Reversal, included in Part 3 of the book *His Kingdom Come: An Integrated Approach to Discipling the Nations and Fulfilling the Great Commission* , (Seattle: YWAM Publishing, 2008), 148–149.
[92] See the Old Testament Template for rediscovering God's principles for discipling nations at: www.templateinstitute.com.
[93] 1 Kings 10:6–7.

Deuteronomy) and set about reforms that transformed the country.[94]

Roman Empire

How were a small group of persecuted, rejected, oppressed and reviled new believers at the birth of the Church in the beginning of the Book of Acts, able to transform a powerful pagan Roman Empire within 300 years with a whole new vision of humanity? The foundation for this remarkable change was a system of beliefs based on a biblical worldview which were revolutionary and unheard of to the people at that time. Contrary to the pagan gods, the Christian God actually loved people and required them to also love others. Whereas cruelty was commonplace in Rome, the Christians worshipped a merciful God who required mercy to be shown to others, including care for the poor. In this new vision of humanity there was to be no cultural, ethnic or class separation. Instead, noblemen and slaves were viewed as brothers! Men were to love their wives and children rather than view them as their own property to do with as they wished without any legal consequences. All of life was sacred, thereby rejecting Roman practices of abortion, infanticide and no regard for those who were handicapped. Furthermore, where pagan physicians would often flee infected cities during an epidemic and the sick were left to die on the streets, the Christian faith stressed acts of charitable love and care to believer and unbeliever alike, including towards those who were sick. The results were profound and caused many who did not believe to turn to the Christian faith. By 300 AD,

---

[94] 2 Kings 22–23.

there were an estimated 6 million Christians, which although only 10% of the Empire's population, led to a transformation of the whole society and culture.[95]

England
A nation builder who had a tremendous impact on the nations was John Wesley. Wesley's effect on Great Britain went far beyond evangelism. His legacy includes contributing to the liberation of women, and the beginnings of workers' rights and safety in the workplace. He attacked slavery before the reformer William Wilberforce[96] was born, fought for civil and religious freedom, brought awareness of the evils of exploiting the poor, opened a medical dispensary, a bookstore, a free school, and a shelter for widows. He also set up spinning and knitting shops and studied medicine in order to help the destitute. In addition, some historians believe that the renewal movement led by the Wesley brothers prevented something similar to the French Revolution taking place in England.[97]

---

[95] From *The Rise of Christianity: How the Obscure, Marginal, Jesus Movement Became the Dominant Religious Force* (HarperOne, 1997) by Rodney Stark, quoted in The Role of the Church in Society by Bob Moffitt (http://harvestfoundation.org/593954.ihtml).

[96] William Wilberforce was a British politician, philanthropist, and the leading abolitionist of the slave trade. It is interesting to note that his conversion led him to question whether he should remain in public life. John Newton, a leading Evangelical Anglican clergyman of the day, former slave-ship captain and author of the hymn "Amazing Grace," counseled him to remain in politics.

[97] A fuller account of John Wesley's impact can be found in Donald Drew's lecture based on the classic 1939 study by J. W. Bready, *England Before and After Wesley*, published in *Missionary Conspiracy: Letters to a Postmodern Hindu* (Mussoorie: Nivedit Good Books, 1996) by Vishal Mangalwadi.

Geneva

John Calvin, along with other reformers at his time, emphasized the need for personal salvation. However, they didn't stop there but taught from the Bible how to reform society. Their goal was to build a city (Geneva) established on the Word of God and during the sixteenth century, they laid a solid foundation teaching biblical principles for social reform, education, government, and economics. The Geneva model would be copied and adapted by many countries as their ideas later spread across northern Europe and to the New World. Max Weber, the German economist, gave credit to Calvin and his teachings and attributed what began in Geneva to be the reason for western prosperity.[98] Loren Cunningham writes:

> Modern economists now have ideas in line with John Calvin, who got his principles from [the Bible]. They will tell you that any country will prosper if it works hard, saves money, makes sure its families stay intact, has reasonable interest rates, and lives under a system of law and accountability. The International Monetary Fund and the World Bank teach some of these principles to the nations. But back in the sixteenth century, John Calvin got these ideas from the Bible.[99]

---

[98] Max Weber, *The Protestant Ethic and the Spirit of Capitalism* (Scribner Library, New York, 1958), quoted in Loren Cunningham, *The Book That Transforms Nations*, 100.
[99] Loren Cunningham with Janice Rogers, *The Book that Transforms Nations: The Power of the Bible to Change any Country* (Seattle: YWAM Publishing, 2007), 90.

Freedom wasn't an accident that happened in Western Europe and North America. It grew out of the teachings of believers who sought the Word of God for principles of government. The Free World owes a singular debt of gratitude to John Calvin and other preachers of the Reformation.[100]

In similar vein, American sociologist, Rodney Stark, writes that without Christianity's commitment to "reason, progress, and moral equality . . . today the entire world would be about where non-European societies were in, say, 1800." This would be a world "lacking universities, banks, factories, eye-glasses, chimneys, and pianos." We could add scientists to that list too.

In his fascinating book entitled *The Victory of Reason: How Christianity Led to Freedom, Capitalism, and Western Success,* Stark further quotes a statement by one of China's leading scholars following comprehensive research into the pre-eminence of the West worldwide. Having become convinced that Christianity is the source of Western prosperity, the Chinese scholars concluded: "The Christian moral foundation of social and cultural life was what made possible the emergence of capitalism and then the successful transition to democratic politics."[101]

Christians were at the forefront of education and in the pursuit of truth with medieval universities such as Bologna, Oxford, Paris, Cambridge, Salamanca, and Padua all being established with an emphasis on Christ and the Bible as the foundations of education. All but two of the

---

[100] Cunningham, 92.
[101] Rodney Stark, *The Victory of Reason: How Christianity Led to Freedom, Capitalism, and Western Success* (Random House Publishing Group, 2005), 235.

first 108 universities founded in America were Christian, including the first, Harvard, which was named after a Christian minister[102] and where the student handbook listed this as Rule #1: "Let every student be plainly instructed and earnestly pressed to consider well, the main end of his life and studies is to know God and Jesus Christ, which is eternal life, John 17:3; and therefore, to lay Jesus Christ as the only foundation for our children to follow the moral principles of the Ten Commandments."[103] Princeton's crest still says *"Dei sub numine viget,"* which is Latin for "Under God she flourishes."[104] In his enlightening book *The Book that Made Your World: How the Bible Created the Soul of Western Civilization,* Vishal Mangalwadi explains:

> Neither colonialism nor commerce spread modern education around the world. Soldiers and merchants do not educate. Education was a Christian missionary enterprise . . . The biblical Reformation, born in European universities, took education out of the cloister and spread it around the globe . . . Western missions birthed, financed, and nurtured hundreds of universities, thousands of colleges, and tens of thousands of schools. They educated millions and transformed nations.[105]

---

[102] Reverend John Harvard.
[103] http://www.faithofourfathers.net/ (accessed 22 August 2011).
[104] http://www.answersingenesis.org/articles/am/v2/n3/harvard-yale-princeton-oxford-once-christian.
[105] Vishal Mangalwadi, *The Book That Made Your World: How the Bible Created the Soul of Western Civilization* (Thomas Nelson Publishers, 2011), 194, 207–208.

In addition to many of the human benefits we perhaps take for granted in Western society, animal protection also owes its beginnings to the work of Christians. In spite of public ridicule and strong opposition in their work for animals, the English Royal Society for the Protection of Cruelty to Animals (RSPCA) came into existence as the result of Christian vision.[106]

There are many other nation builders that could be mentioned including global revolutionary Frank Buchman, and Dutch theologian and prime minister Abraham Kuyper.[107]

Numerous women have also engaged in nation building, such as the English prison and social reformer, Elizabeth Fry. This woman, who since 2002 has been depicted on the Bank of England's five pound note, was the major driving force behind new legislation to make the treatment of prisoners more humane and was supported in her efforts by the reigning monarch, Queen Victoria. She also helped the homeless, establishing a "night shelter" in London, and opened a training school for nurses, becoming an inspiration to Florence Nightingale who is regarded as the pioneer of modern nursing.[108]

---

[106] Reformers William Wilberforce and the Reverend Arthur Broome were instrumental in forming the world's first animal welfare charity in London in 1824.
[107] To read about these men I recommend Jeff Fountain's article, "Revolutionaries and Anti-Revolutionaries: Discipling Nations in the Modern Era," and Thomas Bloomer's article, "Calvin and Geneva: Nation-Building Missions," which are both included in Part 3 of the book *His Kingdom Come: An Integrated Approach to Discipling Nations and Fulfilling the Great Commission*; or *The Book That Transforms Nations: The Power of the Bible to Change Any Country* by Loren Cunningham, both Seattle: YWAM Publishing, 2008 and 2007. Summaries can also be found on my website (www.catalystmin.org) under Nation Disciplers.
[108] en.wikipedia.org/wiki/Elizabeth_Fry (accessed 18 February 2010).

Another example would be the Irish missionary, Amy Carmichael, who spent a lifetime in India working for the dignity and liberation of girls and women being sold into temple prostitution.[109] In 1947, the Indian government made the custom of giving babies and young children to a life as a cult prostitute illegal.

Norway
Over two hundred years ago, a young farm boy in Norway, Hans Nielsen Hauge (pronounced *How-gah*), was given a Bible. Ignoring the government's restrictions which at that time prohibited people to meet in public or travel around the country without permission, Hauge and other lay preachers he recruited were imprisoned many times as they preached and distributed the Bible. In less than three decades, Hauge launched more than one thousand home groups within the state church, in a nation of only 800,000 and wrote books teaching his fellow countrymen to integrate God's principles into every aspect of life, becoming the biggest publisher of his time. In addition he started many businesses and helped direct believers to vocational opportunities in towns where they could make a difference in improving the economy of the entire country. Gradually, as Norwegian believers increasingly influenced their own spheres of the culture they began to disciple society and were positioned to lead Norway as it changed

---

[109] Amy Carmichael (1867–1951) established a home and a school, called Dohnavur Fellowship, for girls she rescued from sexual internment and abuse.

from one of the poorest nations of the world to one of the freest, richest, and most educated.[110]

India

Many Christians are familiar with the "father of modern missions," William Carey. However, Carey was more than just a missionary in the traditional sense. As well as evangelizing the Indian people during forty years of unbroken service, Carey also sought to outwork Jesus' command to "disciple nations"[111] by impacting different spheres of Indian society as follows:

Family–lobbied to see the killing of unwanted babies and the horrific practice of burning widows alive on their husbands" funeral pyres outlawed. These were achieved in 1804 and 1829 respectively;

Religion–started churches which continue to multiply today; founded Serampore College, which trained the first Indian pastors; oversaw the translation of the Bible into nearly forty languages, so that Indians could read it in their mother tongue;

Education–started schools for children of all castes and for women, in addition to Serampore College which became the first liberal arts college in Asia with teaching in vernacular languages;

---

[110] Loren Cunningham with Janice Rogers, *The Book That Transforms Nations: The Power of the Bible to Change Any Country* (Seattle: YWAM Publishing, 2007), chapter 8.
[111] Matthew 28:19.

Celebration (the Arts)–promoted literature by translating and publishing great Indian classics; authored the first Sanskrit dictionary for scholars; elevated the Bengali languages, previously considered "fit only for demons and women," into the foremost language of India; and wrote Bengali ballads to effectively communicate the gospel;

Media/Public communication–brought mass media to India, setting up the first printing press and teaching Indians how to use it, as well as how to make their own paper; established the first newspaper ever printed in an Asian language;

Economy–introduced the idea of savings banks and encouraged reasonable interest rates and foreign investment; introduced the steam engine to India; in medicine led the campaign for humane treatment of lepers, demonstrating a biblical concern for individuals; in science he founded the Agri-Horticultural Society, carried out a systematic agricultural survey; introduced modern astronomy to offset Indians" bondage to astrology; as a dedicated botanist he published India's first books on science and natural history;

Government–in spite of formidable obstacles, given that all missionary activity was banned when Carey first entered India and that the British had done nothing to bring about reform since 1600, he gradually helped bring about a more "civil service" in their colony, and to initiate reforms.[112]

Carey was not only a "Christian missionary," but he was also an industrialist, an economist, a medical humanitarian, a media pioneer, an educator, a moral reformer, and a botanist. It has been said that Carey did more for the transformation of the Indian sub-continent in the nineteenth and twentieth century than any other individual before or since.[113]

South Korea
While there is no nation that has fulfilled its biblical mandate, a modern-day example of a nation that has experienced a measure of transformation through a biblical influence permeating areas of society is South Korea.[114] Remarkably, the number of believers has grown from one half of one percent to at least one third of the country's population in less than one hundred years! The nation now sends thousands of missionaries overseas, second only to the United States. As the church has grown, so has the economy, rising out of the grip of poverty to one of a wealthy nation in only three decades. South Koreans are now at the forefront of technology and manufacturing, exporting cars and electronics. Great progress has also been made in education and literacy. Rather than military rule,

---

[112] Ruth and Vishal Mangalwadi, *The Legacy of William Carey: A Model for the Transformation of a Culture* (Crossway, 1993, 1999).
[113] Mangalwadi, *The Legacy of William Carey*.
[114] Information extracted from chapter 9–An "Overnight" Success Story–from *The Book that Transforms Nations: The Power of the Bible to Change any Change*, by Loren Cunningham with Janice Rogers (Seattle: YWAM Publishing, 2007).

South Korea now has a civilian, democratic government and is seeking to address corruption demonstrated by the conviction of former presidents for abuses of power.[115]

Fiji
Recent events in the nation of Fiji also illustrate what can happen when a nation seeks God to intervene in the affairs of life.[116] After two violent coups in 2000, a national awakening occurred after the Prime Minister and President called for the people of the nation to fast and pray. The spiritual leaders of the different denominations came together, asking one another's forgiveness for malice and slander. In a stunning act of public repentance, the prime minister got down on his knees before the opposition leader, a Hindu, and asked for his forgiveness in respect to the outbreak of Fijian violence in 2000, against the Indo-Fijians (largely Hindus and Muslims). This act of humility led to hundreds of Fijians going to one another in repentance and asking forgiveness. A subsequent Bible teaching program called *Healing the Land* shows numerous converted villages how to live their lives personally and as a community. The spiritual revival is impacting different areas of society. In the capital city most businesses hold regular Bible studies and groups of media professionals are also meeting to understand how to impact their industry.

Perhaps what is the most amazing are the stories from around the country where the environment has experienced a supernatural healing following repentance of

---

[115] It is sobering to note that some of these corrupted leaders were evangelical Christians which highlight the fact that simply having Christian leaders is no guarantee that transformation will occur in a nation.
[116] Cunningham, Chapter 30.

the Fijian people. Water that has been polluted and acidic for more than forty years has become clean and pure again, and coral reef has been restored literally overnight! It is a literal demonstration of 2 Chronicles 7:14, "If My people who are called by My name will humble themselves, and pray and seek My face, and turn from their wicked ways, then I will hear from heaven, and will forgive their sin and heal their land."

The word *land* here is often spiritualized to mean "nation" or "region," but it literally means the ground, the earth, the soil that we grow plants on. It is reported that nations in Africa that have become increasingly Islamic have experienced a dramatic reduction in rainfall.[117] It is therefore important to note that as we consider societal transformation, there is also a correlation with creation which the Bible states is suffering under the weight of the curse of sin and is awaiting the revealing of the sons of God and its ultimate redemption.[118] Part of the cultural mandate is to be good stewards of our environment and planet. Nancy Pearcey, in her book *Total Truth: Liberating Christianity from Its Cultural Captivity,* writes:

> In Genesis, God gives what we might call the first job description: "Be fruitful and multiply and fill the earth and subdue it." The first phrase, "be fruitful and multiply" means to develop the social world: build families, churches, schools, cities, governments, laws. The second phrase, "subdue the earth," means to harness the natural world: plant

---

[117] Cindy Jacobs, *The Reformation Manifesto: Your Part in God's Plan to Change Nations Today* (Bethany House Publishers, 2008), 91.
[118] Romans 8:19–22.

crops, build bridges, design computers, compose music. This passage is sometimes called the Cultural Mandate because it tells us that our original purpose was to create cultures, build civilizations—nothing less . . .

The lesson of the Cultural Mandate is that our sense of fulfillment depends on engaging in creative, constructive work. The ideal human existence is not eternal leisure or an endless vacation—or even a monastic retreat into prayer and meditation—but creative effort expended for the glory of God and the benefit of others. Our calling is not just to "go to heaven" but also to cultivate the earth, not just to "save souls" but also to serve God through our work. For God himself is engaged not only in the work of salvation but also in the work of preserving and developing His creation. When we obey the Cultural Mandate, we participate in the work of God himself, as agents of His common grace.[119]

Such development must be done sensitively and with appropriate care, not exploiting the land or the environment, but acting wisely with due respect towards all of God's creation.

Reading about the great reformers in the past can make our contribution seem insignificant in comparison. The important thing is not to be concerned about the size of our impact but whether we are doing what we can to bring

---

[119] Nancy Pearcey, *Total Truth: Liberating Christians from its Cultural Captivity* (Crossway Books, 2004).

a transforming influence into those spheres of society where we have a voice.

God's perspective is much greater than just seeing people "saved." Being saved is only the beginning. God's heart has always been for nations, to see them discipled and experiencing godly transformation. This task is not just for "missionaries" but for *every* disciple of Jesus Christ.

The apostle Paul writes, "For we are God's workmanship, created in Christ Jesus to do good works, which God prepared in advance for us to do" (Ephesians 2:10). We have been saved and redeemed to do these good works. However, the tendency can be to simply view these "good works" from a Greek dualistic point of view in a narrow and limited spiritual sense only. Don't do that. Remember, it applies to *every* good work!

Local churches can consider the callings of those believers in their communities and leaders can then release them to engage in the different spheres and areas of life. For example, we are to be:

- lawyers seeking truth and justice;
- businesspeople raising issues of ethics in the workplace;
- parents modeling the value of home-making and family while empowering and releasing the next generation;
- scientists revealing the Creator and sustainer of the universe;
- artists, dancers, writers, photographers and film-makers expressing who God is through their creativity;

- medical workers caring for and treating the sick and hurting;
- workers serving to the best of their ability and with a spirit of excellence;
- accountants and auditors ensuring the biblical value of accountability;
- farmers causing the earth to bring forth its bounty;
- conservationists protecting the environment; and
- churches speaking prophetically on great issues[120] and demonstrating the care of the Father in reaching out to the poor, the orphan and the widow.

As every member of the Body begins to serve in their unique gifts and callings, the kingdom of God will come as we work towards seeing King Jesus filling "all in all."

What Discipling a Nation Is Not

It is perhaps important to clarify that when referring to discipling the nations by bringing God's kingdom rule and values into the spheres of society, I am not suggesting that we can expect some perfect utopia on earth. The fullness of God's kingdom will not come until Jesus returns and a new heaven and earth are established, filled with God's glory. However, rather than embracing what has been described

---

[120] Landa Cope makes the point that, whereas today prophecy is often focused on the individual or the church, all of the 17 Old Testament prophets prophesied to nations (*An Introduction to The Old Testament Template*, 155).

as an "eschatological paralysis,"[121] a passive waiting for Jesus' return accompanied by a pessimism that there is little point in challenging the evils around us, we can bring about a foretaste of heaven and demonstrate the blessing of life lived according to God's values.

Similarly, the church is *not* called to take over society and seek to control the other remaining spheres by telling everyone what to do and how to live, or taking away the democratic rights of non-Christians.[122] Jesus should be Lord in all the spheres, with each sphere directly responsible to God. No sphere should overstep its God-given authority in relating to other spheres.[123]

Jesus modeled servant leadership and taught that greatness in God's kingdom comes by serving others. As his people, we are to be salt and light in society, bringing a permeating *influence* like yeast in a loaf of bread, rather than trying to enforce our beliefs on the rest of society in the likeness of a totalitarian regime. North American YWAM leader, Jim Stier writes,

> When we turn away from the methods of our Lord and resort to force, duplicity, violence, or manipulation, the kingdom of God is already dead in us, and we have lost the battle. We must continue

---

[121] Vishal Mangalwadi, *Truth and Transformation: A Manifesto for Ailing Nations*, 213.

[122] This is the position of those who subscribe to a "Dominion Theology" akin to Christian imperialism. Sadly, church history records instances of cultural genocide and oppression, sometimes carried out unwittingly, at other times done mistakenly in the name of Christ.

[123] From the work of Abraham Kuyper discussed in Loren Cunningham, *The Book That Transforms Nations: The Power of the Bible to Change Any Country* (Seattle: YWAM Publishing, 2007), chapter 7.

to serve by the Spirit, in truth, with unrelenting love.[124]

As the church seeks to manifest God's kingdom on earth, there will be many issues which will cause us as Christians to revisit our ethics, our values, and most importantly, to seek God for how his kingdom should be represented and established. The discipling of nations will not be an easy mandate to fulfill. It will stretch us and challenge our well-established patterns of thought and cultural understanding. We will have to learn how to send out "the right message," without compromising biblical values and principles.

A kingdom value is personal freedom and the right to choose the way of life or the way that leads to death.[125] We are to be salt and light, and seek to bring a godly influence which in turn will bless and improve the lives of individuals, their families, their communities, and their nation. The more biblical truth a culture and society embrace, the more it will experience the blessing of God for "righteousness exalts a nation."[126] Conversely, the less a culture holds to a biblical worldview with kingdom values, the more it will suffer the consequences of going its own way.

---

[124] Jim Stier, "Reflections on the Kingdom," in *His Kingdom Come: An Integrated Approach to Discipling Nations and Fulfilling the Great Commission* (Seattle: YWAM Publishing, 2008), 464.
[125] Deuteronomy 30:19.
[126] Proverbs 14:34.

Critical Mass and Prevailing Worldview

To disciple a nation will not necessarily mean that all or even the majority of the people will become Christians. The key issue is what the *critical mass*[127] believes, where a sufficient number of people, when joined together in a common purpose, can cause synergistic results far beyond their numbers.[128] When a critical mass of people has the Bible and applies what it teaches in their lives, a nation is transformed.[129]

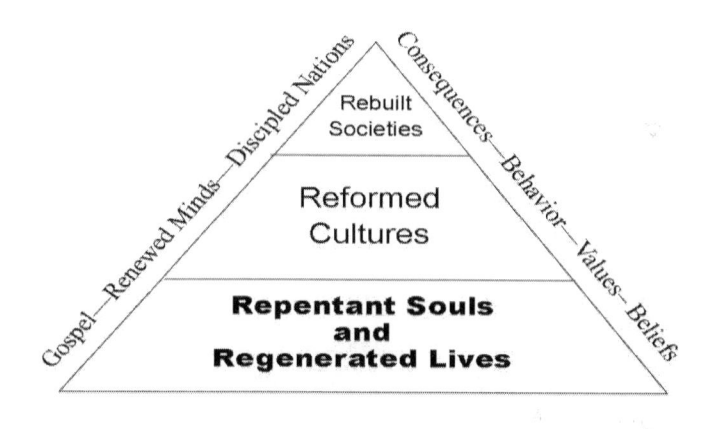

Pyramid diagram: Bottom tier — "Repentant Souls and Regenerated Lives"; Middle tier — "Reformed Cultures"; Top tier — "Rebuilt Societies". Left side label (ascending): Gospel — Renewed Minds — Discipled Nations. Right side label (descending): Consequences — Behavior — Values — Beliefs.

[130]

Societal transformation comes about by *winning the battle of ideas*. It begins by the renewing of our minds and

---

[127] Critical mass is "the minimum amount of fissionable material capable of producing a self-sustaining chain reaction" (The World Book Dictionary, 1978 ed.).
[128] William A. Beckham, *The Second Reformation: Reshaping the Church for the 21st Century*, 222.
[129] Loren Cunningham with Janice Rogers, *The Book that Transforms Nations: The Power of the Bible to Change Any Country* (Seattle: YWAM Publishing, 2007), 18.
[130] Darrow L. Miller, *LifeWork: A Biblical Theology for What You Do Each Day* (Seattle: YWAM Publishing, 2009), 74.

by changing our thinking. The biblical concept of repentance is a complete change of mind. Linking this back to Chapter 1, it is a new way of viewing life, a new worldview.

As local churches commission people into every sphere of society to act as kingdom ambassadors and agents of transformation, Bob Moffitt suggests answers to the following questions should set local church agendas:

What would our village look like if Christ were chief?
What would our city look like if Christ were mayor?
What would our nation look like if Christ were king, president, or prime minister?[131]

In his book *LifeWork,* Darrow Miller refers to Dr. Jun Vencer of DAWN Ministries who believes a discipled nation would be characterized by: economic sufficiency, social peace, public justice, national righteousness, and where all aspects of life are centered around the Lordship of Jesus Christ.[132]

When Christians live and function in their callings from a biblical framework and are like true salt and light, or yeast in bread dough (to use another of Jesus' kingdom analogies[133]), they will begin to permeate, influence, and give direction to the values and focus of the people and

---

[131] Bob Moffitt, *If Jesus Were Mayor: Biblical and Historical Roots of Cultural Transformation Through the Church* (Harvest Foundation, 2005).
[132] Miller, *LifeWork*, 300.
[133] Matthew 13:33, Luke 13:20–21.

culture. Nations are discipled one person at a time.[134] It involves small beginnings, but with large endings. The gospel of the kingdom applied to all areas of life has the power to become the *prevailing worldview* of a people or nation. Where a significant proportion of society functions under the principles of truth and the dominant mind-set of the various spheres of influence is biblical, we can then say that a nation has been discipled.[135]

Expanding our Vision of God

> There is not a square inch in the whole domain of human existence over which Christ, who is sovereign over all, does not cry: 'Mine!'[136]

As we bring the kingdom of God on earth as it is in heaven, he will be seen as Lord over all the spheres:[137]

- Heavenly Father, Comforter—Lord of the Family
- Head of the Body, Great High Priest—Lord of the Church
- King of Kings, Sovereign Servant-King—Lord of Government and Justice
- Great Teacher, Only Wise God—Lord of Education

---

[134] Miller, *LifeWork*, 74.
[135] Dean Sherman, "The Church and the Kingdom," in *His Kingdom Come: An Integrated Approach to Discipling Nations and Fulfilling the Great Commission* (Seattle: YWAM Publishing, 2008), 180.
[136] Abraham Kuyper, former Dutch prime minister and statesman.
[137] List compiled from material produced by The Template Institute and the Discipling Nations Alliance (*www.MondayChurch.org*).

- Potter, Restorer—Lord of the Arts and Beauty, Entertainment and Recreation
- Living Word—Lord of Communication and the Media
- Provider—Lord of Economics
- Designer, Creator God—Lord of Science and Technology
- Healer—Lord of Health
- Architect and Builder—Lord of Infrastructure
- Gardener—Lord of all the Earth
- Love—Lord of Compassion

How big is your God? As you meditate on who God is as Lord over all the spheres of society and every aspect of culture, he will be seen as bigger than ever before. He is the Lord of the Church but his kingdom extends far beyond what we have tended to focus on as being "spiritual." Jesus is so great he cannot be contained in only one area of society. He is to fill *all things* with himself. Everything was created through him and for him, and when the King returns, the glory and honor of the nations will be revealed and celebrated in the new earth.[138]

Simply put, the kingdom of God exists wherever God reigns, *wherever his will and intentions are carried out.* That "wherever" has no limits. He is the Lord of history as well as eternity . . . in the heavens and on the earth . . . over all of his creation. It is he who defines by his very nature what is true, good, and beautiful, and it is for

---

[138] Colossians 1:16-18, Revelation 21:24–26.

this that Jesus told us to pray and work towards . . . his intentions carried out on earth as they are in heaven.

It is for this vision of God's original intent that Jesus lived, worked, suffered, and died. And it is this vision he entrusted to his disciples and the church. This vision, the vision of the kingdom that is "at hand" now, and is also moving toward a time of full realization in all of creation at the end of history, provides the central theme that runs throughout the Scriptures. It is this vision that provides the most powerful symbol of hope in the history of humankind. And it is this vision that should define the whole thrust of our lives as believers. Is such a compelling vision the driving force of your life?

Part 2
Every Believer's Story

CHAPTER 5
THE MISSIONAL CALLING OF THE CHURCH

New Paradigms of Engaging in Missions

At present, our world is changing more rapidly than at any other time in world history. This is not just a result of transitions through the agricultural, industrial, and technological revolutions into the information age, or merely due to the huge impact of globalization. Significant changes have also taken place in the spiritual landscape of our world as well.

In Part 1 we noted that in most churches, missions generally exists (if it does exist at all![139]) as one of a number of projects being run in the church. One of the most significant phenomena in recent church history has been the rapid growth of indigenous missions[140] in the Majority (Two Thirds) World.[141] Beginning in the 1960s and mushrooming in the 1970s and 1980s, today there are more non-Western missionaries than Western missionaries. In addition, the steady decline of Christianity in the Global

---

[139] Sadly, multitudes of churches remain asleep to the task. It is estimated that there are approximately seven Protestant churches in America (the leading missionary sending nation) for every missionary that is sent (Jason Mandryk, *Operation World: The Definitive Prayer Guide to Every Nation*, Biblica Publishing, 2010).

[140] Indigenous missions being native or originating from or belonging to a place, country or culture.

[141] The Majority (Two Thirds) World is essentially Africa, Asia, and Latin America, with 60 percent of the world's population now in Asia.

North is just now being surpassed by the rise of Christianity in the Global South—namely Asia, Africa, and Latin America.[142]

As a follow-up to the world's first global mission conference, which took place in Edinburgh in 1910, four international consultations were held in 2010, bringing together church and mission leaders from around the world. Tokyo 2010 was the first global missions conference organized, conducted, attended, and funded by a majority of non-Western leadership. At the gathering, echoing the Macedonian call recorded in Scripture and lamenting the decline of Christianity in Western Europe, the leader of the Swedish Evangelical Alliance pleaded with the delegates to "Come over and help us!" In response, the director of a Korean mission organization led the assembly to intercede for the peoples of Europe.[143] What a turnaround in one hundred years, from the time when the West was largely Christianized and taking the gospel to the rest of the world!

This shift of Christianity from the Global North southward and eastward has significant implications and impacts how we should view and engage in missions in the twenty-first century. As mentioned in the Introduction to this book, some are referring to a Fourth Wave of missions which will require a renewed way of thinking that expands

---

[142] This is praiseworthy as hundreds of millions heard the good news for the first time in the past century and demonstrates the fruit from missionary efforts over the past two hundred years. Years and generations of prayer and faithful service to the unevangelised world by both missionaries and indigenous Christians have not been in vain (Jason Mandryk, *Operation World: The Definitive Prayer Guide to Every Nation*, Biblica Publishing, 2010).
[143] David Taylor, "Setting the Pace: Tokyo 2010 Leads the Way in Celebrating Edinburgh 1910," *Missions Frontiers*, July—August 2010.

the traditional understanding of "missions," within the context of God's story and his overall mission.

For the Great Commission to be fulfilled, which is the human participation and contribution to the overall mission of God, it will require the effective functioning of the *global* church, east and west, north and south. It will also require *every* believer discovering their place and being released into fulfilling their unique part. Individual callings will vary. Some will involve engagement across cultures, including the more traditional sense of missionary work. For the majority of believers, however, including those who in the past would have dismissed the idea that they had a calling at all, or if they did that it was insignificant and "less spiritual" which has resulted in a disengagement in God's mission, it is time that their callings be affirmed.

> "Just as the Father has sent me, even so I am sending you." (John 20:21, International Standard Version).

God's Mission: At the Core or on the Periphery?

In Part 1 we also saw that in truth, the church exists *because* of its mission—the mission of God (*missio Dei* in Latin). We noted that we are all part of a God-centered drama. History is God's story. Similarly, mission is the outworking of God's story. The gospel is not primarily about us and how we can have our needs met. The gospel is the core ingredient to the mission of God. In the western world we have become so shaped by the culture of individualism that we can easily lose sight of what being a follower of Jesus is really about. Instead of focusing on God's agenda and what he is doing and wants to see accomplished in the world, we can so easily get drawn into pursuing other agendas centered around ourselves, or even the church.

The truth is that God has a mission, global in scope, in which he invites us to participate. This is something bigger than the church, even though God has assigned the church (in all of her different expressions) to be his agent and witness to his purposes in the world. We noted that God's mission revolves around his kingdom being established on earth, under the reign of his King, Jesus Christ. The Gospel writer, Luke, records that during the forty days between Jesus' resurrection and his ascension, of all the issues he could have focused on in his remaining hours on earth, his teaching centered on "things pertaining to the kingdom of God." His disciples were to occupy until he would return again to consummate the kingdom, but to do so they were to wait until they had been empowered by the Holy Spirit.[144] This parallels the parable of the talents that Jesus spoke prior to entering Jerusalem in the run up to his crucifixion, where a certain nobleman (Jesus) was to leave for a far country to receive for himself a kingdom before returning.[145] Luke then records the power necessary for Christ's servants to advance the kingdom in his absence, before setting out the scope and extent of the kingdom on earth.

---

[144] Acts 1:3–8.
[145] Luke 19:11–27.

Every believer can find their place in fulfilling their God-given assignment as part of God's agenda, the Great Commission. This does not mean that every believer should become a missionary in the more traditional sense, quit their jobs and careers, sell everything and move overseas as I did. There is still a need for some to do this. It is important we don't "throw out the baby with the bathwater," which would leave missionaries without the necessary support they need to do what God has called them to. However, every believer and every local community (church) of believers should become *missional* in the way they live their lives.

Adopting Missionary Ways

In John's gospel we read that "the Word became flesh and dwelt among us."[146] The Message Bible paraphrases this verse, "The Word became flesh and moved into the neighborhood." This was God's strategy for revealing himself to humankind. He sent himself, through his Son, Jesus Christ, as his own missionary. God's missionary to earth didn't live in a social "mission compound," detached from the people he had come to. Neither did he erect a special building (as a carpenter he could have built one himself!) and expect people to come to him. He was sent to be among them.

As missionaries moving overseas, the first priority my family and I had to focus on was to begin to study and bond with the new culture. For us this meant we had to learn a new language and seek to build some new

---

[146] John 1:14.

relationships with the people. It would have been futile to arrive with the attitude that the people of the host nation would be automatically open and receptive to the message we were bringing with us. We had to first become students of them as people and of their culture. We had to adopt the attitude of a learner. We had to live among the people and take the time to listen, to observe, and to ask many questions. At the same time, we had to be sensitive to the Holy Spirit and see where God was already at work. While this is good missionary practice in a cross-cultural context overseas, it should be no different in our own cities, communities and neighborhoods, regardless of whether they are multicultural or not. The culture of Christendom once found in Europe and North America has passed away. Western nations now have to be viewed from the same perspective we would take if we went to a foreign land and a culture with which we were unfamiliar. We have to go, observe, listen, and learn. This is the heart of being *missional*.[147]

Being *Missional*

So what does it mean to become missional? As the church in the West wakes up to the reality that the spiritual landscape has changed to one that is post-Christendom, this is a word which has become increasingly popular over recent years but has also led to some confusion as it has been used to mean anything remotely related to evangelism

---

[147] The word "missional" was introduced by a team of authors in *Missional Church: A Vision for the Sending of the Church in North America*, ed. Darrel L. Guder (Grand Rapids: Eerdmans, 1998).

or church growth. Alan Hirsch, a self-described "missional activist" writes,

> A proper understanding of missional begins with recovering a missionary understanding of God. By his very nature God is a "sent one" who takes the initiative to redeem his creation. This doctrine, known as Missio Dei—the sending of God—is causing many to redefine their understanding of the church. Because we are the "sent" people of God, the church is the instrument of God's mission in the world. As things stand, many people see it the other way around. They believe mission is an instrument of the church; a means by which the church is grown. Although we frequently say "the church has a mission," according to missional theology a more correct statement would be "the mission has a church" . . .
>
> . . . many churches have mission statements or talk about the importance of mission, but where truly missional churches differ is in their posture toward the world. A missional community is patterned after what God has done in Jesus Christ. In the incarnation God sent his Son. Similarly, to be missional means to be sent into the world; we do not expect people to come to us. This posture differentiates a missional church from an attractional church.

The church is to be a missional community, based on the missionary nature of God.

> Mission is not merely an activity of the church. Rather, mission is the result of God's initiative, rooted in God's purposes to restore and heal creation. "Mission" means "sending," and it is the central biblical theme describing the purpose of God's action in human history. . . . We have begun to learn that the biblical message is more radical, more inclusive, more transforming than we have allowed it to be. In particular, we have begun to see that the church of Jesus Christ is not the purpose or goal of the gospel, but rather its instrument and witness. . . . God's mission is calling and sending us, the church of Jesus Christ, to be a missionary church in our own societies, in the cultures in which we find ourselves.[148]

Scripture is full of sending language that speaks to God's missionary nature.[149] God the Father sends the Son.[150] God the Father and the Son send the Spirit.[151] God the Father, the Son and the Spirit send the church. For the

---

[148] Darrell L. Guder, ed., *Missional Church: A Vision for the Sending of the Church in North America* (Grand Rapids: Eerdmans Publishing, 1998), 4-5.
[149] For a comprehensive look at sending vocabulary in the Bible, see Alan Roxburgh, *Sending Language* (http://missionalchurchnetwork.com/missional-sending-language/).
[150] In the Gospel of John alone, there are nearly forty references to Jesus being sent.
[151] John 14:26; 15:26; 16:7.

first century Christians, the overriding identity, purpose, and reason for their existence was their "sent-ness."[152]

In their book, *"Introducing the Missional Church: What it is, Why it Matters, How to Become One"*[153], Alan Roxburgh and Scott Boren write,

> God is not interested in getting more and more people into the institution of the church. Instead the church is to be God's hands and feet in accomplishing God's mission. This imagination turns most of our church practices on their head. It invites us to turn towards our neighborhoods and communities, listening first to what is happening among people and learning to ask different questions about what God is up to in the neighborhood. Rather than the primary question being, "How do we attract people to what we are doing?" it becomes, "What is God up to in the neighborhood?" and "What are the ways we need to change in order to engage the people in our community who no longer consider church a part of their lives?" This is what a missional imagination is about.

Being missional therefore requires a whole new way of thinking in line with a biblical worldview and the mission of God. It requires breaking free from old paradigms of spiritual and secular, and of mission being an

---

[152] Darrell L. Guder, *The Continuing Conversion of the Church* (Grand Rapids: Eerdmans, 2000), 186.
[153] Alan J. Roxburgh and M. Scott Boren, *Introducing the Missional Church: What It Is, Why It Matters, How to Become One* (Baker Books, 2009).

activity or outreach program of the church. It is about having a new imagination for being the church, that we are God's *sent* people. It is also the belief that every believer is an agent of God's mission, living as a disciple missionally and incarnationally in their ordinary contexts and spheres of influence.[154] This relates to how we go and what we do as we go. It is recognizing the need to think and act like a missionary who is seeking to enter into the lives of a people who speak a different language and embrace another cultural mindset. It is having an outward-focused, kingdom-oriented discipleship that changes our world.[155]

Forms, Structures, and How We Do Church

As we have seen in considering the full scope of the Great Commission mandate, the church of Jesus Christ is called to engage in both the social transformation of the culture as well as the spiritual transformation of individuals. Major cultural shifts from a modern worldview to a postmodern worldview, along with other changes arising from technological advances, globalization, the breakdown of the family, and the growth of materialism and consumerism, have led many to move away from traditional paradigms of "doing church" to approaches that have a greater focus on experiencing God in the context of an authentic spiritual community, while at the same time engaging the culture and serving the community in which it is a part.

---

[154] For more on how to live missionally, a good resource is *Right Here, Right Now: Everyday Mission for Everyday People* by Alan Hirsch and Lance Ford (Baker Books, 2011).

[155] Alan Hirsch and Lance Ford, *Right Here, Right Now: Everyday Mission for Everyday People* (Baker Books, 2011), 23.

Visualizing the church in new, broad strokes can prove frightening because it takes us above our comfortable surroundings. We are no longer in control. The macro view of the church is as large and encompassing as God Himself, and stretches us beyond our limited time/space dimensions. It takes us far above the safety of our logical physical world into God's spiritual realm of vision and faith. . . . Simply changing materials, programs and activities is not enough. We must change how we perceive the church, how we see God expressing Himself in the world through the church, and how we do church.[156]

A shift from the "traditional church" and "contemporary church" models (which began with the church growth movement and includes the seeker-church movement) to a more recent paradigm which is described by a number of labels (but not synonyms) including "organic church,"[157] "emerging missional" church, "transformissional" church, "non-institutional church," and "simple church," is one response which will have implications on how church and mission is done in the

---

[156] William A. Beckham, *The Second Reformation: Reshaping the Church for the 21st Century* (Touch Publications, 1995), 13.

[157] T. Austin-Sparks first coined this term and, according to Frank Viola, it relates to a nontraditional church that is born out of spiritual life instead of constructed by human institutions and held together by religious programs. See Frank Viola, "What Is an Organic Church? A Plea for Clarity," *Beyond Evangelical*, http://frankviola.org/2010/01/11/what-is-an-organic-church-a-plea-for-clarity/ (last accessed January 17, 2012).

future.[158] Such church forms are in some instances more akin to house church movements which have grown over recent decades in parts of the world, including within China, and will tend to resonate with those growing up in a postmodern generation who will be less loyal to denominations and institutional structures that were accepted by previous generations. This emerging generation believes Jesus intended his followers to interact with the culture around them rather than becoming an alien subculture.[159] It is noteworthy that "fresh expressions of church" is a term coined by the Church of England report "The Mission-shaped Church" and used in the Church of England and the Methodist Church since 2005.

Institutionalism is an issue that does not just apply to older, denominational structures. It can apply to newer church forms too as communities of believers increase in size. What matters more is the effect of such growth. In the fledgling stage, mission tends to be a priority, but in time, unless recognized, the priority can become preservation and maintenance, which in some instances can require large amounts of money to keep the church "in business."

> A complete paradigm shift is essential for the Western church to avoid becoming an anemic shell of its former self. If we have any realistic hope of

---

[158] For more detailed study there are a growing number of books available on non-institutional forms of church such as Alan Hirsch, *"The Forgotten Ways: Reactivating the Missional Church"* (Grand Rapids: Brazos Press, 2006); Frank Viola, *"Reimagining Church: Pursuing the Dream of Organic Christianity"* (David C. Cook, 2008) and Neil Cole, *"Organic Church: Growing Faith Where Life Happens"* (Jassey-Bass, 2005).

[159] Marcia Ford, "The Emerging Church: Ancient Faith for a Postmodern World"(www.explorefaith.org/ford/emerging.html (last accessed January 17, 2012).

recovering the Christian witness in the West, the church must abandon the diluted role and shortsighted vision as a static institution and dive headlong into its original calling as a missionary movement.[160]

Another recent development has been the emergence of the Internet church or cyberchurch, a blogging movement which religious pollster and author George Barna sees as one of the future "macro-expressions" of church in the future, one that will soon account for one-third of American spirituality, together with other "revolutionary" forms of church. He predicts that "millions of people will never travel physically to a church, but will instead roam the Internet in search of meaningful spiritual experiences."[161] Andrew Careaga, author of *eMinistry: Connecting with the Net Generation*, writes:

> We should not allow cybercommunities to replace the existing Christian communities of the church, but they can become extensions of the church into the online world. We should neither reject the virtual world altogether nor strive to escape our physical world by creating some parallel "online" life. Instead, we should strive to integrate valuable attributes of cyberchurch into our offline lives and

---

[160] Alan Hirsch and Lance Ford, *Right Here, Right Now: Everyday Mission for Everyday People* (Baker Books, 2011), 64.
[161] George Barna, *Revolution* (Tyndale House, 2005).

our offline faith and values into our online encounters.[162]

In the West the issue of an appropriate form and structure applies equally to both the church and the mission agency. Tough questions will need to be asked, and mere survival can never be a vision for the future and will not be sufficient to enter meaningfully into what God is doing in these days.

> The biggest mistake that the Western missionary movement can make is to act as though [nothing ever changes]. Over a quarter of a century on, the world is a different place. In another 25 years, it will be a different place again. Only as we respond to and embrace the changes in our culture, and accept the strengths and gifts of each generation, can the church truly be a place and a messenger of reconciliation, for all generations, in a changing world.[163]

In my own mission organization, Youth With A Mission, one new initiative is The Tribe. This grassroots movement seeks to connect those who have in the past been a part of YWAM but are now working and living in all areas of society. Through reconnecting with some three million people who have been trained with YWAM and

---

[162] Andrew Careaga, *eMinistry: Connecting with the Net Generation* (Kregel Academic and Professional, 2001), 170.
[163] Richard Tiplady, "Let X=X: Generation X and World Mission," in *Global Missiology for the 21st Century*, William D. Taylor ed. (Grand Rapids: Baker Academic, 2000), 475.

have the organization's DNA imprinted in them but are no longer connected with the global mission, The Tribe is a vehicle that is aimed at mobilizing these people by creating missional communities within their homes and spheres where they are working, so that they can live out their lives for nation discipleship and transformation, and be trained in community to disciple others through the Internet.[164]

Contextualization

Donald McGavran, missionary to India and father of the modern Church Growth movement, highlighted the importance of establishing strategic "bridges of God" to counter the social barriers that exist when reaching out across other cultures. McGavran also saw the dangers of "extractional evangelism"; in endeavors to Christianize a whole people, the first thing not to do is snatch individuals out of their society and put them into a different one. Such sentiments are behind the "insider-movements," currently proving very fruitful in outreach among Muslims, Buddhists, and Hindus.[165] Similarly, in the post-Christendom Western context where the church has largely lost the high ground it once had, the necessity for contextualizing the gospel will encourage a missional approach of engaging with neighboring communities.

---

[164] For more information see www.ywamtribe.com.
[165] According to Rebecca Lewis, an "insider movement" is any movement to faith in Christ where (a) the gospel flows through pre-existing communities and social networks, and (b) believing families, as valid expressions of the body of Christ, remain inside their socio-religious communities retaining their identity as members of that community while living under the Lordship of Jesus Christ and the authority of the Bible. See *International Journal of Frontier Missiology*, Summer 2007, 75.

A number of references have already been made in this book to postmodernism, which although still in its infancy has now become the prevailing culture in the Western world.[166] As previously stated, postmodernism is a tendency in contemporary culture characterized by the rejection of objective truth and much of what related to "the modern era" or "modernism."[167] Christians, churches, and mission organizations must be willing to be perceived as "trouble-makers" or counter-cultural. In an attempt to remain relevant and credible and even ensure survival, some churches shift with the prevailing culture and end up conforming to the culture. As a result we see that the church today has succumbed to or mimicked postmodern culture in that less than 20 percent of Christians believe in absolute truth and morals. Rather than to be fashioned by the world, we are to be shaped by the kingdom culture of timeless truth, beauty, and goodness, not adapting *to* culture but representing kingdom culture in a relevant way *within* our existing culture. This includes communicating the gospel in a culturally appropriate way.

In commenting on the issue of cross-cultural communication, Lesslie Newbigin writes:

> Neither at the beginning, nor at any subsequent time, is there or can there be a gospel that is not embodied in a culturally conditioned form of words.

---

[166] Given that modernity took nearly two centuries to find its full expression in the Enlightenment and rationalism we can expect the postmodern philosophy to also take time to understand its full implications.

[167] Modernism was the predominant cultural movement since around the year 1500 which emphasized analysis and objective truth. It gave rise to the nation-state, organized and institutional religion, the pursuit of machines, consumerism and the market economy.

The idea that one can or could at any time separate out by some process of distillation a pure gospel unadulterated by any cultural accretions is an illusion. It is, in fact, an abandonment of the gospel, for the gospel is about the word made flesh. Every statement of the gospel in words is conditioned by the culture of which those words are a part, and every style of life that claims to embody the truth of the gospel is a culturally conditioned style of life. There can never be a culture-free gospel.[168]

Newbigin's statement that there can never be a culture-free or pure gospel is worth repeating. History has demonstrated the ease in which the gospel and culture can be entwined. For missionaries going to foreign lands, it has always been a challenge to leave "cultural baggage" behind and not export the sending nation's ways along with the message of good news. We have distorted the meaning of incarnational mission when as Western missionaries we have imposed our own denominational templates on less developed nations and transposed our Western cultural expressions in the place of local ones. North China missionary, Roland Allen, highlights the dangers of paternalism in his classic book entitled, *Missionary Methods: St. Paul's or Ours?*:

> We have simply transplanted abroad the [church] organization, with which we are familiar at home... When native leaders finally are ready to take

---

[168] Lesslie Newbigin, *Foolishness to the Greeks: The Gospel and Western Culture* (Grand Rapids: Eerdmans, 1986), 4.

charge, the system will proceed precisely as it did before, natives simply doing exactly what we are now doing.[169]

This warning is not solely applicable to church-planting missionaries. With modernization making most nations multiethnic, it is incumbent upon all believers and churches to "bridge the gap" by contextualizing the gospel and being incarnational witnesses to the truth and freedom found only in Jesus Christ. At the same time, we need to speak biblical words into a culture. In some tribes in Africa, they have no word for "woman." This shows how the cultural story and value system does not even value women as human beings. The gospel and church taken to that culture has not sought to change it appropriately and thus the language. As a result, the gospel simply becomes an overlay of animistic tribal beliefs and values.[170]

Multiplying, Indigenous Churches

Using botanical imagery, the term "indigenous church" refers to a church that arises from the soil of its own society. It is native to the culture, abidingly relevant and powerful, influencing entire communities with the life of the kingdom of God.[171] For this to occur, missionaries must resist the tendency to want to control national churches or creating dependency through outside funding or other

---

[169] Roland Allen, *Missionary Methods: St. Paul's or Ours?* (Grand Rapids: Eerdmans, 1912, 1962), 180.
[170] Darrow Miller, personal e-mail correspondence, June 7, 2011.
[171] "Spontaneous Multiplication of Churches," lesson 13 in *Perspectives on the World Christian Movement Study Guide*, (William Carey Library, 2009).

missionary care. Instead, as the apostle Paul demonstrated,[172] emerging local church leadership can be recognized, affirmed, and developed,[173] and the church commended to the power and care of the Holy Spirit, and released to reproduce and influence their society.

For those engaged in church planting in their own nations, it is vital that churches continue to grow to avoid stagnation and eventual decline. Many who are committed to growth seek to do so through addition rather than multiplication. However, if we are to see a completion of the Great Commission, it will be imperative that churches adopt a New Testament multiplication model, where existing churches continue to multiply by sending out and reproducing other communities of believers.

Are all Christians "Missionaries"?

At the risk of repeating myself, the purpose of this book is to demonstrate that *every* believer is called and has a unique role in the fulfillment of the Great Commission— God's invitation for humankind to join him in contributing to his story and mission on planet earth. But does this mean that every Christian believer is a missionary?

As I remarked in Chapter 2, there are some who are now saying that this is so. In a sense this may be true as the

---

[172] Paul typically stayed with a new church for three to five months before moving on to the next place, an exception being at Corinth where he remained eighteen months (Acts 18:11).
[173] Church-planting trainer, George Patterson, sees the church-planting missionary essentially as a trainer, with the discipling relationship between missionary and leader being a model for new church leaders to follow. The author received training from Patterson during a YWAM School of Frontier Missions in 1995.

English word *"missionary"* is derived from Latin and is the equivalent of the Greek-derived word, "apostle," which means "sent one." All Christians have been *sent* into the world[174] and hopefully by now you will have recognized that God desires *every* believer, in *whatever* spheres of life, to intentionally *engage* in doing their part of the Great Commission to teach and disciple nations. However, just as all Christians are exhorted to evangelize does not mean that every believer is an "evangelist." Some specifically have this gift and calling. The same could be said of pastoring and teaching. We all during the course of our lives care for others and teach, but this does not mean we are called to be pastors or teachers.

In the same way, while every believer is called to engage in God's mission, some are called to cross-cultural missionary work, which requires adequate preparation and training for it to be effective and fruitful. It also requires adequate and knowledgeable missionary care that addresses the unique challenges associated with cross-cultural work. Without these things, both the senders and those being sent may end up disappointed. Furthermore, the unique challenges missionaries engaged in cross-cultural work experience cannot be overlooked. These may include adjusting to another culture, language acquisition, raising children overseas, fund-raising, along with the unique stresses, sacrifices and costs involved with leaving family and all that is familiar and normal back home. Without adequate support and care, those being sent may also end up being damaged.

---

[174] See John 20:21.

While scholars might want to argue over terminology, I see the traditional use of the word "missionary" as applying to the trained *cross-cultural worker* who reaches out to a certain people or part of the world God has called him or her to. As we will see in the next chapter, cross-cultural work is one of many equally valid and valuable callings and vocations. Most believers are not called to the unique work of a "career" missionary who as part of their calling will become bi-cultural, but every believer is a witness and can and should be *missional* (with a clear sense of being called and sent on a mission) in carrying out God's unique calling and gifting in their life.

CHAPTER 6

THE CALLING OF EVERY BELIEVER

At the beginning of this book I highlighted that surveys indicate that most Christians feel disempowered. For some, they feel that unlike those called to be pastors, missionaries, or some other form of church work, they are of little use to the kingdom of God. This is vitally connected to the fact that many Christians do not feel any sense of calling from God.

> If you're a Christian in a "secular" job, have you sometimes wondered if you've missed God's best? Should you have gone overseas as a missionary? Or served as a church pastor? Did you fail to hear "the call"? This occupational inferiority complex infects believers around the world. It can keep you from doing your everyday work "wholeheartedly, as to the Lord." Although no heavenly voice called Daniel to government work in Babylon, he served God in that role—and did so full time.[175]

The question is never, "Am I called to ministry?" but "To which ministry am I called?"

As this book has sought to repeatedly emphasize, God desires the active and intentional involvement of *every* member of Christ's body in the Great Commission. All

---

[175] Larry Peabody, *Job-Shadowing Daniel: Walking the Talk at Work* (Outskirts Press, 2010), 13.

Christians, not just religious workers, have a calling. This isn't just about what we do, but relates to hearing and responding to what God communicates with us and calls us to. There is firstly a *general* call to Jesus Christ and to enter the kingdom, making him Lord and receiving life through God's gift of salvation. Secondly, having been called into the kingdom, there is a *particular* calling which is our unique work assignment to manifest and advance God's kingdom in the earth.

For some people these callings may be communicated through a dramatic encounter with God, such as Saul's "Damascus road" experience, Isaiah's vision of God on a highly exalted throne, or Moses' "burning bush." My wife, Michelle, had a very dramatic conversion experience (her primary general call into God's kingdom). Some may receive their particular calling in a dramatic way too. However, this is more of an exception than the rule. For most people, including some of the most devoted servants of God in the Bible, such as Daniel and Esther, their sense of calling doesn't come with awesome special effects but comes through a growing conviction over time. As Oswald Chambers wrote, "The realization of the call in a person's life may come like a clap of thunder or it may dawn gradually."[176]

God calls people on an individual basis. All work, not just spiritual work, can be considered a calling. So let's now consider issues that relate to our calling.

---

[176] Oswald Chambers, "The Awareness of the Call," in *My Utmost for His Highest*
(http://utmost.org/the-awareness-of-the-call/) (accessed 15 August 2011).

Living Before an Audience of One

Whereas the dualistic paradigm (considered in Chapter 2) separates the spiritual from the physical and secular, and in so doing makes a distinction between those who are engaged in "spiritual" work (e.g., pastors, evangelists, missionaries) and those who are in "secular" work, a biblical worldview supports no such way of thinking. While our gifts and callings are different, some callings are not superior or more spiritual than others. Whatever our calling and vocation in life, we are to live twenty-four hours a day, seven days a week, living and working as an act of worship before God. Rather than the nature of one's work, it is the faith with which one works that matters. There is no separation between the sacred and the secular. The secular dwells in the presence of the sacred. The secular is infused with the sacred.[177] Our forefathers in the faith used a Latin phrase, *coram Deo,* meaning "before the face of God," to describe this way of life. Others refer to the concept of "the audience of one."[178] This is a lifestyle that is lived in the presence of God, the one who sees all, knows all, and desires for his people to live and abide with him 24/7.

There is, however, a distinction between living a consecrated life or an unconsecrated life. As highlighted in Chapter 3, the Protestant Reformation challenged this dualistic worldview that had crept into the church during the Middle Ages and stressed that all work, provided it was not evil but consecrated before God, was sacred and of

---

[177] Miller, *LifeWork,* 65.
[178] For example, Os Guinness, *The Call: Finding and Fulfilling the Central Purpose of Your Life* (W Publishing Group, 1998, 2003), Chapter 9.

equal value. A consecrated life is a life lived *coram Deo,* with God first place and in worship for the glory of God alone. An unconsecrated life is where a person lives as a Christian only when "in church" on Sundays or when it is convenient. One person may be a godly auto mechanic while another is an adulterous evangelist. One may be a godly farmer while another is a corrupt pastor or businessman.[179] In these instances, the mechanic and farmer are "more spiritual" than the evangelist and pastor.

Living an Integrated Christian Life

As Darrow Miller explains in his excellent book *LifeWork: A Biblical Theology for What You Do Every Day,* we are not called to live in two different worlds, or live two different lives. All of life, including the hours of my work, is to be lived *coram Deo,* for the advancement of God's kingdom, for the glory of the Lord of heaven and earth.

The following diagram is helpful to show that regardless of a person's vocation, recognizing that for some their "occupying territory" for Christ and his kingdom will involve cross-cultural "deployment," the key and correct distinction that can be made is whether we are living a consecrated or an unconsecrated life.

---

[179] Miller, *LifeWork,* 66.

Living in ONE World

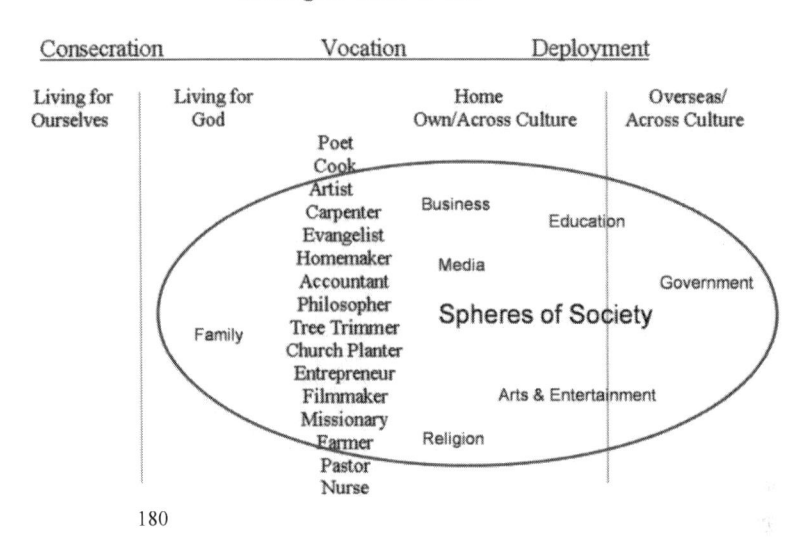

Consecration	Vocation	Deployment
Living for Ourselves / Living for God	Home / Own/Across Culture	Overseas/ Across Culture

Family

Poet
Cook
Artist
Carpenter
Evangelist
Homemaker
Accountant
Philosopher
Tree Trimmer
Church Planter
Entrepreneur
Filmmaker
Missionary
Farmer
Pastor
Nurse

Spheres of Society: Business, Education, Media, Government, Arts & Entertainment, Religion

For the Christian believer, *every* area of life should be an act of worship, not just what happens within the confines of a church meeting. This has been made possible through the Cross when Jesus restored meaning and purpose to our work lives so that they could once again be a way to worship God.[181] Brother Lawrence, a monk in the 1600s whose job was dishwashing, learned this important truth that even in the midst of seemingly mundane tasks, he could experience the presence of God as when he was on his knees in prayer.[182] Similarly, in the movie, *Chariots of Fire,* Scottish Olympic runner, Eric Liddell, expressed this

---

[180] Adapted graphic from Darrow L. Miller, *LifeWork*, 65.
[181] It is worth noting that the English terms in the Old Testament for "work" and "worship" both come from the same Hebrew word, "avodah".
[182] Brother Lawrence, *The Practice of the Presence of God (*Revell Publishers, reprinted edition 1967).

concept well with his words, "When I run I feel his (God's) pleasure."

Have you ever thought about the fact that the Savior of the world spent the majority of his adult life in his earthly father's "secular" carpentry business? Even after he began his travelling ministry, over 90 percent of his public appearances were in the marketplace and forty-five of the fifty-two parables Jesus told had a workplace context.[183] What is important is engaging in God's mission and a key to doing this is discovering who God has made you to be and then being released into expressing God through your life!

> As believers, our engagement with the world is determined to a large extent by our specific callings in life—our vocations. We have the opportunity to examine our lives, understand our gifts, and recognize God-given opportunities to exercise them for the advancement of his kingdom. Most Christians will be called into small arenas, where we exercise some degree of influence. By God's grace we have the ability to mature in our abilities for the glory of Christ and his kingdom.[184]

Rather than viewing work occupations like a kind of football league table indicating varying degrees of "spirituality," with the role of "church leader," "pastor," or "missionary" as being "premier league" occupations, compared to other work roles filling in the slots in the

---

[183] Os Hillman, *The 9 to 5 Window: How Faith Can Transform the Workplace* (Regal Books, 2005), 23.
[184] Miller, *LifeWork*, 208.

lower divisions, every Christian should find joy and freedom to do what God has uniquely called them to do. Our God-given gifting and calling is not necessarily to be worked out within the context of the church/mission sphere. This is just one sphere (which can be labeled "Religion") and will therefore only equate to a certain part of the body of Christ who are appointed by God to focus in this domain. Most believers will be called to one or more of the other spheres. If you are called to the business world, your purpose is not solely to finance the preaching of the gospel or the next church building program. This might be a part of it, but there will be other things related to the economic sphere that God may ask you to do in terms of bringing a biblical worldview and modeling kingdom business run on godly values and principles (I will return to seeing business as mission later in this chapter). Gifted teachers and educators are not to be limited to Sunday school programs, and accomplished musicians and communicators should not feel that they are only using their talents for God if they are involved in a worship service or producing the church bulletins each week. At the entrance of one church I know, they have a banner which the congregation can see as they leave the church premises. It reads: "You are now entering your mission field!" What a great perspective to have for the remaining six days of every week.

In the past, due to a dualistic worldview, the church has largely stayed away from being an influence in major areas of society. Some spheres have been viewed as being too worldly or even evil. In some countries Christians will not even cast their vote in an important national election because they believe politics to be "of the devil." For too long, Satan has been given too much slack by the church to influence and bring a needed contribution in many significant spheres of life, particularly in the entertainment industry, the arts world, media and communications, and politics. I am not suggesting that the church should be overseeing or ruling in these different arenas. However, Christians across the globe should be actively engaged in every area and bringing a positive "salt and light" ingredient and demonstration of the kingdom of God in each and every one.

> "Let me tell you why you are here. You're here to be salt-seasoning that brings out the God-flavors of this earth. If you lose your saltiness, how will people taste godliness? You've lost your usefulness and will end up in the garbage. Here's another way to put it: You're here to be light, bringing out the God-colors in the world. God is not a secret to be kept. We're going public with this, as public as a city on a hill. If I make you light-bearers you don't think I'm going to hide you under a bucket, do you? I'm putting you on a light-stand. Now that I've put you on a hilltop, on a light stand—shine! Keep open house; be generous with your lives. By opening up to others, you'll prompt people to open up with God, this generous Father in heaven." (Matthew 5:13–16, The Message)

> "Whatever you do, work at it with all your heart, as working for the Lord, not for people, since you

know that you will receive an inheritance from the Lord as a reward. It is the Lord Christ you are serving." (Colossians 3:23–24)

A Biblical Theology of Work

I remember in the 1980s reading the book *Secular Work Is Full-time Christian Service* by Larry Peabody.[185] The author's message was directed at those believers who considered themselves second-class citizens in the kingdom of God because their daily calling was to be worked out in the "secular" world. He sought to demonstrate that serving God in business was not any less spiritual than serving God in "full-time ministry" (which incidentally is a misnomer as all Christians should be "full-time," living for God 24/7), and that boredom and frustration could be exchanged for joyful fulfillment in the marketplace. This book was seeking to restore a truth that was rediscovered during the Protestant Reformation but is still often lacking today. It sought to address the split thinking that had crept into the church from the time of Augustine (AD 354–430) that wrongly divided life into what is "sacred" (or spiritual) and what is "secular" (or non-spiritual).

A more recent book which seeks to help every Christian reconnect their lives and work with God's plan for individuals, communities, and nations is a book I have already referred to by Darrow Miller, *LifeWork: A Biblical Theology for What You Do Every Day*.[186]

---

[185] Larry Peabody, *Secular Work Is Full-Time Service*, retitled *Serving Christ in the Workplace* (Christian Literature Crusade, 1980, 2004).
[186] Darrow L. Miller, *LifeWork: A Biblical Theology for What You Do Every Day* (Seattle: YWAM Publishing, 2009).

Calling and Vocation, Career and Job

Now that we have considered the importance of living wholistically in whatever vocation God has called us to, it is perhaps helpful to make the distinction between our vocation (calling) and any career or job we may be engaged in.

Vocation—this is the "big picture" and is derived from the Latin word *"vocare"* which means "to call." Our vocation must incorporate our "calling," "purpose," "mission" and "destiny." It is what you are doing in life that makes a difference, that builds meaning for you, and that leaves a legacy. Our vocation and calling is when we discover our part in God's story.

Career—this is a subset of vocation, a line of work which will be a part of fulfilling one's calling. Where a series of jobs have a common thread, each one is often seen as a step towards forming a career. Careers can change during a lifetime and there will be several careers that fulfill any "vocation."

Job—the most specific and immediate of the three terms. This is what you do daily to produce an income. A job will ideally be part of your calling but at times may not be directly related to it. Most people will have several different jobs in their lifetime, but changing or losing one's job should never change your "calling."[187]

---

[187] "Is Your Job Your Calling" by Dan Miller (http://www.48days.com/store/calling/).

Business as Mission

"Business as mission" is a relatively new phrase, but the idea is an old one. Throughout church history businessmen and women have carried the gospel along with their trade to other nations. However, business as mission is gathering fresh momentum in the emerging Fourth Wave. There is a growing wave of Christians who are recognizing they are called to business as a vocation, and as a result seek to integrate their faith and business life, and to use for-profit business development as an instrument of wholistic mission to the world.

It is important to note that this is not "ministry" tacked on to business for convenience or business tacked on to ministry. Instead, the mission is carried out in and through the business, through its activities, through the products and services, and through relationships. Business has tremendous potential as a force for good, to tackle poverty, to stimulate local economies, to bring social and environment improvements, and to carry the message of eternal hope to people and places which are often otherwise beyond reach. Furthermore, because a profitable business is self-sustaining, it can help to bring about sustainable social, economic, environmental, and spiritual transformation. Those who are engaging in this exciting new development recognize that the purpose of church, missions, and business is the same—to demonstrate the kingdom of God.[188]

---

[188] For more information see www.businessasmission.com.

Kingdom Transformation through Wholistic Living

Whether in the marketplace or in some other area of society, it is exciting to see being restored to the body of Christ worldwide the truth that for the believer, *all* of life is to be regarded as "spiritual." It has the potential to release every member of the body into a biblical view of their work and fruitful and effective service in every sphere of life and society in which they have an influence. This will come about as part of a lifelong process. It will take time and prayer to discover how God's kingdom can and should be established in each of the spheres. It will come about as we also seek to understand God's priorities and what he wants done.

In referring to the need for wholistic transformation of the whole of society and the whole of this world, Ralph Winter writes of the importance of believers to be ever mindful of God's agenda:

> Evangelicals today, now with far greater wealth and influence, need to realize that heightened privilege calls for expanded and more complex responsibility. The amount of money Bill and Melinda Gates are putting into the defeat of malaria is no more than peanuts compared to the funds Evangelicals annually fritter away on non-essentials. Yet no respectable, organized effort of Evangelicals now exists that is stepping up to bat to seek the eradication of diseases that afflict millions, including millions of Christians. Does the conventional message of churches today challenge

followers of Christ to deliberately choose microbiology as well as "Christian ministry"? (Note that Kingdom Mission means more than "social action" if it is to eradicate disease germs. The Bible speaks of restoration not just social action.) Come on! Can't we digest the fact that thousands and thousands of Christian families around the world are, right now, so poor and diseased that when they can't feed their children they must sell them into forced labor for them to be able to eat? In Pakistan hundreds of thousands fall into this category. Half of such children die by age 12.

Doing lots of good things, or as someone has said, "Keepin' busy for Jesus" individually may be a case of "good but not good enough."[189]

Every Believer Has a Personal Mission Field

As a missionary who has lived overseas, in returning to the West I have sometimes been asked if I will once again return to "the mission field." While I understand what is being meant, this question comes from a faulty dualistic paradigm that sees missions as only taking place overseas, preferably in a far and distant land. Without invalidating the specific work and calling of missionaries (see page 114), if we refer back to the diagram above, our "mission field" could be either at home or in another culture, depending upon our place of deployment. Whereas the term

---

[189] "Three Mission Eras," Chapter 41, *Perspectives on the World Christian Movement* (William Carey Library, 2009), 278.

"mission field" has traditionally been associated with the work of missionaries, as every believer finds their place in advancing the kingdom as part of the Great Commission, they will also discover (in line with the church banner mentioned previously) that they too have a mission field or place of deployment, wherever that may be.

CHAPTER 7
THE COMMISSIONING OF EVERY BELIEVER

Before my family and I left England to go to China for the first time, we were commissioned by the leaders of two churches. Hands were laid on us, prayers offered, prophetic words uttered, and the anointing of the Holy Spirit requested for the task that God had called us to. This time of "sending out" was a great encouragement to us and many Christians will be familiar with this kind of commissioning for those embarking on missionary service. Similarly, such practices are commonplace for those "entering the ministry" in other kinds of church work. We typically have times of "ordination" for new church leaders, ministers, elders, and maybe deacons. Commissioning those who are to serve in these roles is important and necessary. However, the fact that these believers are usually the only ones in a church community who are commissioned in this way is further evidence of the dualism that is embedded into much of our thinking and church practices. Church leaders, pastors, and missionaries are seen as having important and special tasks to perform for the kingdom of God, and are thus commissioned by the rest of the Body. True, but so does everyone else!

The New Testament simply does not speak in terms of two classes of Christians—"minister" and "laymen"—as we do today. According to the Bible, the people (laos, "laity") of God comprise all Christians, and all Christians through the exercise of spiritual gifts have some "work of ministry" [Ephesians 4:12]. So if we wish to be biblical, we will have to say that all Christians are laymen (God's people) and all are ministers. The clergy-laity dichotomy is unbiblical and therefore invalid. It grew up as an accident of church history and actually marked a drift away from biblical faithfulness. A professional, distinct priesthood did exist in Old Testament days. But in the New Testament this priesthood is replaced by two truths: Jesus Christ is our great high priest, and the Church is a kingdom of priests (Hebrews 4:14; 8:1; 1 Peter 2:9; Revelation 1:6). The New Testament doctrine of ministry rests therefore not on the clergy-laity distinction but on the twin and complementary pillars of the priesthood of all believers and the gifts of the Spirit. Today, four centuries after the Reformation, the full implications of this Protestant affirmation have yet to be worked out. The clergy-laity dichotomy is a direct carry-over from pre-Reformation Roman Catholicism and a throwback to the Old Testament priesthood. It is one of the principle obstacles to the Church effectively being God's agent of the Kingdom today because it creates the false idea that only "holy men," namely, ordained ministers, are really qualified and responsible for leadership and significant ministry. In the New Testament there are functional distinctions between various kinds of ministries but no hierarchical division between clergy and laity.[190]

Traditional ordination concepts contradict the New Testament and help to perpetuate the "clergy-laity," "spiritual-secular" divisions, along with reinforcing the idea that some Christians are called to ministry while others are not. If given the opportunity, I suspect many churches would grab the opportunity of having a pastor like the British nineteenth century preacher, Charles Haddon Spurgeon, still known as the "Prince of Preachers," or Dwight L. Moody, who some claim to be the greatest evangelist of the nineteenth century, to lead their churches. But did you know that neither of these men was "ordained"?

In the New Testament where the word "ordain" is used,[191] the meaning relates to the recognition, endorsement and affirmation of the work of God in someone's life, someone who is already functioning in their gifting; rather than setting an individual into an "office" or endowing them with special status, thus creating a special, professional caste of Christian.[192] In the true biblical sense of the meaning, every believer can be "ordained" and commissioned in their God-given gifts, life purpose and calling.

---

[190] Howard Snyder, *The Community of the King* (InterVarsity Press, 1977), 94–95.
[191] The Kings James Version translates "ordain" from a number of Greek words and uses the term more than other translations. The word also has a Latin root (*ordinare*) related to Roman law and appointments to the Roman senate.
[192] For a fuller account of the historical roots of the modern day practice of ordination, see *Pagan Christianity? Exploring the Roots of our Church Practices*, by Frank Viola and George Barna, Barna Books, 2008.

By the fourth century, the ceremony of ordination was embellished by symbolic garments and solemn ritual. Ordination produced an ecclesiastical caste that usurped the believing priesthood. From where do you suppose the Christians got their pattern of ordination? They patterned their ordination ceremony after the Roman custom of appointing men to civil office. The entire process down to the very words came straight from the Roman civic world.[193]

In his booklet *Supporting Christians at Work*, London Institute of Contemporary Christianity executive director, Mark Greene, refers to a full-time school teacher who receives prayer at the front of the church in order to spend an hour each week teaching Sunday school, but not for the teaching she does the rest of the week.[194] Similarly, members of the congregation who are about to go on a short-term mission trip will often be called to the front and prayed over, but what they do the majority of their lives in the routine of "normal" life and work is never recognized, validated, and prayed over.

Just imagine how exciting and empowering it would be if *every* believer in a local church community had the opportunity of being prayed for, commissioned, and sent out into their particular spheres of influence in society. There would no longer be scores of believers feeling disempowered in church meetings, feeling that their

---

[193] Viola and Barna, 124–125.
[194] Mark Greene, *Supporting Christians at Work* (Administry and LICC, 2001), 5.

vocation in life was unspiritual, and that what they spend the majority of their waking hours and years of their lives doing is insignificant for the kingdom of God.[195]

For this to occur, a new way of thinking will be necessary. A biblically informed view of work and vocation will be required. Some churches run courses to help people in their congregations to identify their spiritual gifts so they can find their place and become more effective within the ministries of the church. This is good but it will not by itself address the reasons why many Christians feel disempowered in church. This is because the majority of believers are not called to work within the confines of a church setting. They need to be helped to discover and identify their true callings and God-given passions, and then affirmed and released into whatever God has put in their hearts to be and do, in whatever spheres of influence that will take them. It is into these callings within the marketplace, within the political world, the educational world, the world of the arts and entertainment, the family, or wherever it may be, that each and every believer should be commissioned. "Each Christian is to be ordained for his or her ministry, to be set apart for the assignment given by Christ. The church is to release each person into his or her destiny."[196]

In their book *Untamed: Reactivating a Missional Form of Discipleship*, Debra and Alan Hirsch tell a story of how they "commissioned" the entire congregation of South Melbourne Restoration Community, one Sunday morning,

---

[195] We spend 50 to 75 percent of our waking hours and 60 to 90 percent of the years of our lives working.
[196] *LifeWork*, 316.

At South we took the "priesthood of all believers" (that every person is a minister and needs to be released as such) seriously. This didn't mean that our community always lived this out, but it was a value we tried to live by (and at times used humor to reinforce). In order to drive this point home, one Sunday morning, as our community arrived for our gathering, we greeted each person at the door and handed them a two-inch-wide strip of white flexible card and a fastener. Many looked puzzled but decided to play along, wondering just what we were up to.

A short time after the service began, Al asked everybody to stand up and fasten the white strip around their necks. He then proceeded to lead the whole church through an ordination ceremony. It wasn't quite what people were expecting, but that morning each and every person gathered at South was officially ordained into the ministry of Jesus. Once they were all ordained, they could dispose of the symbolic (and very unnecessary) dog collars and just live out their commission.[197]

Why Commission Every Believer?

Why should your church even consider commissioning people in their everyday jobs? Here are some reasons:

---

[197] Alan and Debra Hirsch, *Untamed: Reactivating a Missional Form of Discipleship* (Baker Books, 2010).

Firstly, *validation*. Every believer needs to understand that whatever their vocation and calling, it is of value and worth to the kingdom of God. They need to know that as they live their lives for God, using their gifts and passions for his kingdom, their work and efforts bring God pleasure and contribute to the completion of the Great Commission. Such validation also reinforces a biblical worldview and theology of work, and tears down a disempowering dualistic and Gnostic mindset.

Secondly, *affirmation*. Christian believers "out there" in the various spheres of society need to have their work affirmed by their brothers and sisters in Christ. Much encouragement and strength can be gained from the public confirmation of individual callings, especially when surrounded all week by unbelievers living from an entirely different worldview and set of values.

Thirdly, *support*. Public commissioning can aid the understanding and involvement of others, especially in prayer. Increased awareness of each others' vocations and spheres of influence may also lead to groups forming for mutual prayer and support, and possible strategizing for advancing God's kingdom.

Fourthly, *empowerment*. Having been validated and affirmed, and with the support of others, every believer can be sent out with a clear sense of empowerment, with the knowledge that they are no longer mere spectators in church or second-class citizens in the kingdom of God, but ambassadors and change agents for the King!

Let the commissioning of *every* believer begin!

CHAPTER 8
THE EQUIPPING OF EVERY BELIEVER

God has appointed and anointed some within his body with equipping gifts. In the Bible, these are described as apostles, prophets, evangelists, pastors, and teachers. In line with all good leadership practice, these giftings are not intended to result in the leaders doing everything or controlling others, but rather to release and empower the rest of the body to be all they have been anointed to be.

> The modern Western church is like a football match with 22 people on the field in desperate need of rest and 50,000 people watching from the sidelines in desperate need of exercise.[198]

> "And He Himself gave some to be apostles, some prophets, some evangelists, and some pastors and teachers, *for the equipping of the saints for the work of ministry* . . ." (Ephesians 4:11–12, italics mine)

Given the clarity of this verse of Scripture, it begs the question why so many Christians feel they are in passive mode while a relatively small number of believers do the "work of ministry." A primary purpose of those believers called and gifted to function within the religious

---
[198] Linus J. Morris, *The High Impact Church: A Fresh Approach to Reaching the Unreached* (Gospel Light, 1993), 168.

sphere of church and mission—apostles, prophets, evangelists, pastors, and teachers—is to equip the church. Those with these gifts and callings are not more important than the rest of the body. They just have a different function and calling within the body which is to equip and empower other believers for ministry within their areas of life influence and across the spheres of society. So let us now consider issues which relate to how every believer can be equipped to function effectively in their callings.

Disciples making Disciples

> Sitting in a pew watching the paid staff put on a Sunday morning show is all too often the American view of discipleship; this view is not biblical, and it is killing the Church.[199]

The Great Commission has a clear component of discipleship. Whether discipling individuals or nations, the process of learning is integral to becoming like Christ and living according to God's ways. Right from the beginning, humankind has had the command to multiply.[200]

> "You therefore, my son, be strong in the grace that is in Christ Jesus. And the things that you have heard from me among many witnesses, commit these to faithful men who will be able to teach others also." (2 Timothy 2:1–2)

---

[199] The view of Jim Putman and Real Life Ministries as cited in Lisa Sells, Avery Willis' "Last Dream," *Mission Frontiers*, January–February 2011.
[200] Genesis 1:28.

Jesus gave us a clear relational model to imitate in how he discipled by not only preaching to the crowds but also investing in the personal development of twelve individuals.[201] Eleven of them would become the nucleus to seeing God's mission multiplied throughout the world. Did you know that if every Christian were to lead one person to Christ every year and disciple that person so that they in turn would do the same the next year, it would only take approximately thirty-five years to reach the entire world for Jesus? As church planter and pastor Neil Cole writes:

> Has the thought ever occurred to you that we are only one generation away from extinction? If we all failed to reproduce ourselves and pass the torch of life into the hands of the next generation, Christianity would be over in just one generation. Yet, because of the POWER of multiplication, we are also just one generation away from worldwide fulfillment of the Great Commission—the choice is ours.[202]

The failure of the church (especially in the West) to equip most followers of Jesus to reproduce their faith in the lives of others is considered to be one of the most troubling obstacles to world evangelization today.[203] While many pastors and church leaders are close to burnout, the majority of church members do not see that God has any

---

[201] *The Master Plan of Evangelism* (Revell), by Robert E. Coleman is a classic on the method of Jesus and the true nature of discipleship.
[202] Multiplying on the Micro Level: We Each Began as a Zygote, by Neil Cole (http://www.cmaresources.org/node/183—accessed 11 May 2011).
[203] A Discipleship Revolution: The Key to Discipling all Peoples, by Rick Wood, *Mission Frontiers* January-February 2011, 4.

other role for them except as spectators.[204] The result is not only the lack of exponential growth which arises from reproducing disciples, but more fundamentally the fact that much of the Church remains in passive mode, feeling disempowered and lacking in vision that their lives could count for any greater significance than Sunday church attendance.

Every Believer Equipped for Service

A document written in 1945 with the title *Towards the Conversion of England* stated: "We are convinced that England will never be converted until the laity use the opportunities daily afforded by their various professions, crafts and occupations." Organized religion in the United Kingdom has severely declined to the point where it is generally overlooked and ignored.[205] Like the frog that is put in a pan of warm water but doesn't realize that the heat is gradually being turned up, much of Western society is becoming increasingly secularized. The warning issued in *Towards the Conversion of England* in 1945 has not been heeded and what is being witnessed today is in part due to the fact that the Church has not equipped or commissioned those who have the ability to impact their spheres of influence for Jesus Christ.

> Relatively few churches and pastors are reinforcing the legitimacy of a call into so-called "secular

---

[204] Wood.
[205] Religion in the United Kingdom: Diversity, Trends and Decline, by Vexen Crabtree, 2007 http://www.vexen.co.uk/UK/religion.html (accessed 20 Feb 2010).

work." I have colleagues with tremendous business influence who are starving spiritually in their local churches. There's zero feeding; there's zero reinforcing of the call they have in the marketplace.[206]

How many times have you heard a sermon devoted to the subject of work? According to Os Hillman, surveys reveal that more than 90 percent of church members in the United States do not feel they are being equipped by the Church to apply their biblical faith in their daily work life.[207] In the UK, 47 percent of Christians say that the teaching and preaching they receive is irrelevant to their daily lives.[208] It is the least relevant where people spend most of their time—in the workplace. According to research by the London Institute of Contemporary Christianity (LICC), 50 percent of Christians have never heard a sermon on work and 75 percent have never been taught a biblical view of work or vocation. LICC executive director, Mark Greene writes:

> There is a danger that we will view church members exclusively in terms of how they can contribute to the church in the neighborhood, rather than how they might also contribute to the growth of the kingdom of Christ, wherever He has placed them.

---

[206] John D. Beckett (http://www.christianitytoday.com/ct/2007/february/31.124.html) (accessed 15 August 2011).
[207] Have you Noticed? America is being Secularized, article by Os Hllman, http://www.intheworkplace.com/apps/articles/default.asp?articleid=16372&columnid=1935
[208] Mark Greene, *Supporting Christians at Work* (Administry and LICC, 2001).

> Do we run the risk of letting our desire to build a strong local church distract us from asking how God might want to use our people outside our local context?[209]

On highlighting the importance of churches including in their preaching schedules relevant vocational teaching, Darrow Miller writes,

> The cause of Christ can advance more during six days of the week than on Sunday, more in the marketplace than in the walls of the church building. Because of this, we need to spend more time teaching on subjects of the kingdom and vocation than on the solely "spiritual" focus found in so many churches.[210]

A biblical theology of work and vocation must not only be preached from the pulpit; it must also be outworked in a very practical way that prepares and equips believers to be the people God has called them to be and function in their spheres of influence. Most Bible studies are focused on helping us function spiritually, but it is vital to also "equip the saints for the work of ministry" in the marketplace and every other area of society too! Christians from individual spheres (e.g., Christian educators, businesspeople, politicians, parents) could gather to seek God together for strategic and impacting ways to bring a kingdom influence and apply biblical truth and principles

---

[209] Greene.
[210] *LifeWork*, 316.

within their particular spheres and communities. Local churches could run workshops to help Christians learn how to connect their work to the kingdom of God. In his book, *Stretch*,[211] Gerard Kelly dreams of a church where there are "prayer meetings for dentists and think-tanks for nurses; where teachers meet to talk together of the kingdom possibilities in their schools; where people who have known success in business take time to mentor and equip the unemployed; where artists and photographers and DJs and web designers seek each other out to create vital sparks of prayer and interaction."[212]

> The domains of society are in need of kingdom leadership that manifests the true nature and purposes of God and his creation. The work of the church is twenty-four hours a day, seven days a week, not just Sundays. It is in the world, not in a building. The work of the church is to bring the kingdom mind and value systems into the world, not the world's mind and value system into the church. When a critical mass of members of Christ's body embrace their callings as his ministers and are equipped to live and work in the world as incarnational communities, truth, goodness, and beauty will flow with liveliness from the church

---

[211] Gerald Kelly, *Stretch: Lessons in Faith from the Life of Daniel* (Authentic Publishing, 2005).
[212] Included in Larry Peabody's blog, Meshing Sunday and Monday: Commissioning (http://www.calledintowork.com/articles/article.asp?articleID=72) (accessed 15 August 2011).

into the community and nation. Through Christ's body, God will make himself known.[213]

As Christians around the world embrace their God-given destiny and are *released* in confident ministry where they are for the majority of their waking hours, this will, in turn, usher in a new move of God across the spheres of society. In the words of evangelist and Christian statesman Dr. Billy Graham, "I believe one of the next great moves of God is going to be through believers in the workplace." Christian researcher, George Barna, writes, "Workplace ministry will be one of the core future innovations in church ministry."[214]

As a tool to help Christians recognize where the most unreached peoples in the world are located, we have what is known as the "10/40 Window," the area of land between the lines of latitude ten degrees and forty degrees north of the equator, stretching from northern Africa to east Asia.[215] It has been suggested that given the amount of time Christians spend in the workplace, perhaps the "9 to 5 Window" is the greatest mission field in the world. It certainly presents an exciting window of opportunity!

Diaspora Ministry—People on the Move

Equipping Christians in how to bring God's kingdom into the marketplace and other areas of society is certainly one key area in which the church needs to develop. Another

---

[213] *LifeWork*, 317.
[214] George Barna with Mark Hatch, *Boiling Point: Monitoring Cultural Shifts in the 21st Century* (Regal Publishing, 2003), 253.
[215] See *www.1040window.org*.

crucial area is to train and equip believers in cultural awareness and to reach out cross-culturally within their own local communities and workplaces.

> "From one man he made all the nations, that they should inhabit the whole earth; and he marked out their appointed times in history and the boundaries of their lands. God did this so that they would seek him and perhaps reach out for him and find him, though he is not far from any one of us." (Acts 17:26–27)

People today are on the move! In our smaller, "borderless" world, one in thirty-five people are now international immigrants. Globally, 3 percent of the world's population lives outside their homeland, with an escalation in numbers and scope in the last three decades. Around the globe, 200 million people now live and work outside their homeland. God is moving people around demographically and moving them spiritually to be receptive to the gospel.[216] The Church has a unique opportunity in accomplishing God's mission to reach and disciple the diaspora[217] people. Dr. Sadiri Joy Tira, Lausanne[218] Committee for World Evangelization's senior associate for Diasporas writes, "One need not look further than the local Starbucks to meet Diaspora peoples. They are studying in our school, drinking coffee at our cafes, serving our meals at our favorite Sunday restaurants, playing with the kids in

---

[216] www.conversation.lausanne.org/en/home/diaspora.
[217] "Diaspora" is a Greek word meaning "dispersion or scattering."
[218] Lausanne is a worldwide movement that mobilizes evangelical leaders to collaborate for world evangelization (*www.lausanne.org*).

our playgrounds, and jogging around the park with us. They may even be living 'next door.'"[219]

"*Diaspora*" is a Greek word meaning "dispersion or scattering." In today's globalized world, peoples are being dispersed and scattered for a number of reasons including:

- International travelers for study, business, tourism, or labor migration
- Political refugees of conflict
- Displaced populations due to disasters, or
- A community experiencing social transition due to new cultural trends[220]

Diaspora mission is not to replace traditional and other mission initiatives but is certainly a growing paradigm in response to the new demographic reality of the 21st Century. Not only does it present an unprecedented opportunity to reach out *to* the diaspora right outside our front door, it also has the immense potential of ministering *through* the diaspora. Those within diaspora churches can be challenged to reach out to those in the post-Christian West, along with sending diasporic groups back to their homelands to engage in mission. Many who come for international study later return to take up key positions of influence back in their home countries.

Approximately 260 of today's world leaders (that's more than 40%) received their college education within the

---

[219] www.southasianconnection.com/articles/547/1/Diasporas- People-on-the-Move/Page1.html
[220] Globalization, Diaspora Missiology, and Friendship Evangelism by Tuvya Zaretsky (included in Lausanne World Pulse May 2010, 5).

United States.[221] In the past, overseas students who spent time in the West and later became very significant leaders back in their home countries include China's former Communist Party leader Deng Xiaoping, the Vietnamese Community revolutionary leader Ho Chi Minh, and Pol Pot, leader of the Cambodian communist movement the Khmer Rouge. Just think how the destinies of these men and of their nations could have been different had they been exposed to the gospel during their time abroad.

Today, Chinese overseas students number more than 180,000 per year[222] and this annual figure is expected to increase to 300,000 by 2020.[223] Unfortunately, the majority of international students and refugees are never invited into the home of their host nation.[224] Notwithstanding, up to 10 percent of returning students do so as Christian believers! As I write this section of the book here in Vancouver, I'm aware that there are over 17,000 Mainland Chinese arriving in Canada to study every year.[225] Sometimes when walking through a local shopping centre or taking a stroll through a public park at the weekend, the number of Asian faces I see makes me feel like I am living back in China!

---

[221] U.S Department of State's Bureau of Education and Cultural Affairs (quoted in Lausanne World Pulse May 2010 by Dr. Douglas Shaw, president/CEO of International Students, Inc.).
[222] 180,000 students left China to study overseas in 2008 (Xinhua 26 March 2009).
[223] Cheng Li 2007:7 (asiapolicy.nbr.org).
[224] 75 percent of international students and 80 percent of all refugees living in the U.S. are never invited into an American home! (Sources: Douglas Shaw, president/CEO of International Students, Inc. and www.globalfrontiermissions.org/refugees.html).
[225] Study permits issued to Mainland Chinese for 2009, http://www.asiapacific.ca/statistics/immigration/education/study-permits-issued-applicants-asia (accessed 8 September 2011).

Diaspora mission, or glocalized[226] evangelism, as it is sometimes referred to, is a tremendous opportunity to build relationship with those coming from often "closed" nations overseas. This can be done by offering to teach your native language, hospitality, home stays, and simply reaching out with acts of Christian kindness and love. The effectiveness of this kind of ministry can be greatly enhanced as people are equipped to reach out cross-culturally. Missionaries and mission organizations will be key resources within the Body of Christ to help in this regard.

Justice and Compassion

To see societal reformation and transformation through the permeation of the core values of the kingdom of God—beauty, wholeness, security, opportunity, prosperity, reconciliation, and justice—it will be essential that Christians are encouraged and equipped to be 'salt and light' and for influential works of service in their communities and the world.

> "He has showed you, O man, what is good and what does the LORD require of you but to do justly, to love mercy, and to walk humbly with your God." (Micah 6:8)
>
> The calling to "do justice, love mercy, and walk humbly with God" is for every believer. Thus,

---

[226] "Glocal" is a term combining global and local, reflecting the fact that the nations and cities of the world are increasingly inhabited by peoples from many cultures, ethnicities, and races.

Christians must give deep thought and prayer about how each of us can live out this calling as we use our vocational talents and interests.[227]

"I was hungry and you fed me,
I was thirsty and you gave me a drink,
I was homeless and you gave me a room,
I was shivering and you gave me clothes,
I was sick and you stopped to visit,
I was in prison and you came to me."
(Matthew 25:35–36, The Message)

    Since the birth of the church, Christians have been active in reaching out to the poor with charitable acts and practical expressions of God's love. Motivated not only by the Great Commission but also by the Great Commandment—to love God and one's neighbor[228]—the necessity of such acts of kindness and service have helped shape the world conscience about the poor and needy today. Scripture is full of exhortations to engage in "mercy ministry" and to respond to the needs of the poor, afflicted, and disadvantaged. While church history contains periods where Christians have debated the merits of a "social gospel," such tangible expressions of the kingdom of God will only increase as we fully embrace the mission of God.

    In spite of the tremendous technical advances and economic growth witnessed in recent decades, much of the world's population is largely untouched by such modern developments. Many have also become part of the price

---

[227] http://www.trevecca.edu/academics/programs-departments/center-for-social-justice
[228] Matthew 22:37–39, citing Deuteronomy 6:5 and Leviticus 19:18.

and social ills that go hand in hand with these advances, particularly in large urban areas. There is therefore a need for ministries of mercy and justice in the social, political, and economic arenas of life, more than at any previous time in history.[229] Steve Goode, vice president of YWAM Mercy Ministries International, writes:

> Our world is confronted today with two billion people living in or just above absolute poverty, global health issues and disease, under- or unemployment, children at risk, family breakdown, war, terrorism, and crime. God is not silent. He hears and he weeps. He is moved. He acts, sometimes supernaturally, but mostly by using ordinary people. He sent Jesus as a compassionate, loving response. Today, Jesus' words to us ring loudly, "As the Father has sent me, I am sending you" (John 20:21)—to love individuals, families, and communities who have not heard.[230]

Introducing kingdom values and a biblical worldview is an integral part of bringing good news to the poor. As noted in Chapter 1, how a person views the world will shape their beliefs about everything.

> Refugees, orphans, widows, prisoners, the sick, the poor, the lonely, the destitute, and the elderly often

---

[229] Justice meaning equal justice before the law, based on the fact that all people are made in the image of God and are thus equal before God and the law, rather than a view of social justice meaning "equal economic outcomes".
[230] G. Stephen Goode, "Loving God and Your Neighbor: The Influence of Charity and Mercy Ministry upon Society," in *His Kingdom Come* (Seattle: YWAM Publishing, 2008), 296.

have several things in common. They are vulnerable, often afraid. They feel alone, unloved, and without value. They live without hope, are uncertain about today and even more so about tomorrow. Some have survived or continue in situations of terrible abuse, fear, or oppression. They may wonder, Is this my karma? Am I cursed by the spirits? Is this God's will?

We followers of Jesus have a message of good news to the poor. Transformation begins by the renewing of our minds, by changing our thinking. It is not enough just to put faith in Christ. We must seek to have his mind and his thoughts about our world. We must try to view the world through *his* eyes. Proverbs tell us, "As a man thinks in his heart, so is he" (Prov. 8:37 KJV). The poor have an even more desperate need to understand their history, their value, their self-worth and human dignity, and the true basis of their identity. When this occurs, the gospel really does become good news.[231]

There are many ways of engaging with and empowering the poor and needy. Examples include microenterprise development (loans to the poor for small businesses), primary healthcare and community development, ministry to children at risk, orphans, homeless, refugees, HIV/AIDS education and prevention, emergency relief.

---

[231] Ibid., 301–2.

Furthermore, as kingdom agents, we are also to take a stand, raise our voices, pray and act over the injustices in our world. One of the most serious issues is gender injustice—the abuse and suppression of women[232]—which can be seen in many forms, such as domestic violence, prostitution, rape, pornography, and human trafficking (sometimes called the "largest slave trade in history"), to name just a few.

Through mercy ministry, providing hope and human dignity, and standing against evil and injustice, individuals can be transformed, communities impacted, and nations discipled in the ways of God.

Sending and Support

Every believer will require support to be who God has called them to be. This will include moral and prayer support, and possibly other ways depending on the need. As missionaries, my family and I have a team of supporters—ministry partners—who support us in prayer, financially, and through communication. However, whatever our vocation and calling in life, we all need other people who know us, will care for us, and to share life with. We all need community, intimate allies and "fellowships of the heart" that are outposts of the kingdom, those who will fight for one another and for what God has called us to.[233]

---

[232] Darrow L. Miller with Stan Guthrie, *Nurturing the Nations: Reclaiming the Dignity of Women in Building Healthy Cultures* (Paternoster, 2008), addresses one of the greatest causes of world poverty: the lie that men are superior to women.

[233] For more on this I recommend chapter 11, Fellowships of the Heart, in the book, *Waking the Dead: The Glory of a Heart Fully Alive*, by John Eldredge (Thomas Nelson Publishers, 2003).

This is vital when we recognize the spiritual warfare that we are all engaged in (more on this in the Conclusion).

Multicultural Leadership and Teams

Over the past 100 years Christianity has experienced a profound shift in its ethnic and linguistic composition. In 1910 over 80 percent of all Christians lived in Europe and Northern America. By 2010 this had fallen to less than 40 percent, with the majority of Christians located in Africa, Asia, and Latin America.[234] With this shift in Christianity's center of gravity towards the east and south, it is certain that in the future a greater degree of leadership will come from Christian leaders in these parts of the world.

Working together in multicultural settings will necessitate a growing understanding of each other's cultures and the impact they have on how we think and behave. Multicultural teams can give rise to many benefits such as modeling the diversity of the body of Christ, demonstrating God's transforming power in intercultural relations and the healing of the nations, and a heightened sensitivity as to what is biblical and what is cultural. However, there are also potential pitfalls relating to issues such as how team members from different cultures express themselves, defer to leadership, deal with confrontation, view relationships, personal space and lifestyle, and the values that are considered most important.[235]

---

[234] Todd M. Johnson and Kenneth R. Ross, editors, *New Atlas of Global Christianity* (Edinburgh University Press, 2009).
[235] See The Potential and Pitfalls of Multicultural Mission Teams by David Greenlee, Yong Joong Cho and Abraham Thulare, *International Journal of Frontier Missions*, 1995, vol. 12, 179–183.

Without an understanding of the concept of "power distance," intercultural tensions will inevitably arise.[236] Power distance refers to the lack of familiar relationship between the levels of authority, such as teacher and student, officer and soldier, boss and employee, even parent and child. Usually, the more formal the society, the greater the distance between authority figures and their subordinates.[237] "High power distance" cultures, where hierarchy is accepted as normal, tend to be found in the non-Western world. "Low power distance" cultures would include Anglo-Saxon, Scandinavian, and other northern European nations. Richard Tiplady writes,

> In international or multicultural contexts, people from "high power distance" cultures tend to act as though they are powerless, whereas those from "low power distance" cultures behave as though they have power. The result? The latter (usually Westerners) dominate the discussions and the planning, whereas the former appear to sit back and let them.[238]

Adopting an attitude of a learner, patient understanding and a reliance on the work of the Holy Spirit will be essential to overcome the cultural barriers that will otherwise abort the realization that unity in diversity is

---

[236] For further study I recommend Eric Law's book, *The Wolf Shall Dwell with the Lamb* (Chalice Press, 1993), and *Foreign to Familiar: A Guide to Understanding Hot- and Cold- Climate Cultures* by Sarah Lanier (McDougal Publishing, 2000).
[237] Lanier, 92–93.
[238] Richard Tiplady, *World of Difference: Global Mission at the Pic "N" Mix Counter* (Paternoster Press, 2003), 168.

achievable and is something that should be valued and pursued.

Use of Technology

Technological advance has helped pave the way for God's mission to progress. Beginning with how the early Church used the Roman roads and common Greek language to advance the gospel, Ron Boehme, in his assessment of the "waves" of mission, highlights the following examples:[239]

First Wave—the Age of Exploration and invention of the compass and other navigational techniques, took missionaries by ship to the coastlands of the world, while Gutenberg's printing press in 1450 led to a wider distribution of the Bible and other Christian literature

Second Wave—the Industrial Revolution brought new machinery, travel on steam or coal-based ships, advances in medicine, and better living standards allowing increased giving to mission causes

Third Wave—an explosion of wealth and technology including commercial plane travel, with the Information Age resulting in rapid advances in the use of radio, television, cable, fiber optics, computers, cell phones, the Internet and the worldwide web, making much of the world a global village.

---

[239] Ron Boehme, *The Fourth Wave: Taking Your Place in the New Era of Missions* (Seattle: YWAM Publishing, 2011).

As the Fourth Wave emerges, the Church worldwide has more resources and technology than at any time in history to take the gospel to all peoples and see the kingdom of God extended throughout the earth. Many of the barriers that existed before have now been removed through modern forms of communication. With computer software technology, human languages can now be translated in months rather than years[240] and information can be communicated around the world in seconds. Tools such as 4K global mapping[241] help provide data on where the unreached and the most pressing needs exist on the planet. In the new Digital Age in which we now live, most of the world's population has a mobile phone and along with technologies such as online chatting, instant communications can take place between people all across the globe.

A new mission field now resides in your home through the Internet and the World Wide Web. Google and other companies are providing the infrastructure, but "all things were created by him and for him."[242] As a global communication network which will connect everyone on earth is being created, we are witnessing how "the gospel

---

[240] New technologies mean that Wycliffe Bible Translators original estimate that it would take until 2150 to have a portion of Scripture translated into every one of the world's 6,900 spoken languages, has now been brought forward to 2025–an advance of 125 years!

[241] Like a Christian version of Google Earth, 4K is a map which provides a new way to see the world and respond to their needs by creating 4,000 geographic areas called "Omega Zones" (they are called Omega Zones because the final goal is to see Jesus, the Alpha and Omega, represented in every part of the earth). Strategic information can be easily accessed such as those living in absolute poverty, the homeless or the unemployed, those struggling with life addictions, women and children at risk, and those who have been sexually abused, trafficked or enslaved (*www.4kworldmap.com*).

[242] Colossians 1:16.

of the kingdom will be preached in the whole world as a testimony to all nations, and then the end will come."[243] Consider the following:

- China will count approximately 1.3 billion mobile subscribers by 2014.[244]
- Mobile cellular subscriptions worldwide are increasing rapidly and currently stand at over 5.3 billion.[245]
- India has set a deadline of May 2012 to provide broadband access to every village with a population of more than 300 people.[246]
- O3b Networks mission is to make the internet accessible and affordable to those who remain cut off from the information highway.[247]

Walt Wilson, who is a past and present board member of many Silicon Valley corporations and a former managing director of Apple Computer's US Operations, estimates that by 2015 there will be WiFi[248] everywhere on earth. Furthermore, he believes that with the use of the Internet, combined with mobile devices, there will be no

---

[243] Matthew 24:14.
[244] http://techcrunch.com/2010/03/18/soon-therell-be-more-mobile-web-users-in-china-than-people-in-the-united-states/(accessed 16 May 2011).
[245] http://www.itu.int/net/pressoffice/press_releases/2011/15.aspx (accessed 16 May 2011).
[246] http://www.timesonline.co.uk/tol/news/world/asia/article7057435.ece (accessed 16 May 2011).
[247] O3b is short for the "Other Three Billion," the nearly half of the world's population that has little access to the Web (www.o3bnetworks.com).
[248] The term WiFi suggests Wireless Fidelity. A Wi-Fi enabled device can connect to the Internet when within range of a wireless network connected to the Internet.

barrier to reaching the world for Christ by 2020. In his speech at Biola University's inaugural annual Imagination Summit, the founder and chairman of Global Media Outreach[249] remarked that in the next several years, technology will enable the gospel to be available in every person's living room, car, office, pocket, purse or grass hut. Furthermore,

> Our generation has within its grasp everything that is required to fulfill the Great Commission. . . . I believe that God has built this network to accomplish that very purpose [reaching the entire world] within our lifetime. We are the first generation in all of human history to hold within our hands the technology to reach every man, woman, and child on the earth by 2020. We are being called to engage in the battle for human souls, all across the world. We are being given the tools to meet them in their time of need. The moment they step out of the darkness, we are there to meet them. . . . We have to get our people out of the pew and into the battle, and this is the tool to do it.

God has given the church what it needs to complete the task of the Great Commission. Innovative and responsible ways of utilizing what is available will be

---

[249] Global Media Outreach, a division of Campus Crusade for Christ, is one example where the Internet is being used as a communications platform for the gospel. Their website reports that fifteen million people indicated decisions for Christ in 2010 (www.globalmediaoutreach.com/about_us.html).

required to help make the Fourth Wave a tsunami wave of blessing to all peoples and nations.[250]

In Luke 19 Jesus tells the parable of the minas or talents.[251] His purpose was to instruct his disciples about the kingdom of God and about how we have all been given and entrusted with certain gifts, abilities and opportunities for us to steward and be responsible for. One day we will have to give an account when he returns.

> "While they were listening to this, he went on to tell them a parable, because he was near Jerusalem and the people thought that the kingdom of God was going to appear at once. He said: "A man of noble birth went to a distant country to have himself appointed king and then to return. So he called ten of his servants and gave them ten minas. "Put this money to work," he said, "until I come back."
>
> But his subjects hated him and sent a delegation after him to say, "We don't want this man to be our king."
>
> He was made king, however, and returned home. Then he sent for the servants to whom he had given the money, in order to find out what they had gained with it.
>
> The first one came and said, "Sir, your mina has earned ten more."

---

[250] New media tools and advancing technological developments are required to present the gospel to oral learners, those who cannot or will not read and rely on spoken communications. According to Global Recordings, oral learners make up some 75 percent of the world's population (http://globalrecordings.net/en/vision) (accessed 30 August 2011).

[251] Also sometimes referred to as the parable of the gold coins or the pounds. A similar parable is recorded in Matthew 25:14–30.

"Well done, my good servant!" his master replied. "Because you have been trustworthy in a very small matter, take charge of ten cities."

The second came and said, "Sir, your mina has earned five more."

His master answered, "You take charge of five cities."

Then another servant came and said, "Sir, here is your mina; I have kept it laid away in a piece of cloth. I was afraid of you, because you are a hard man. You take out what you did not put in and reap what you did not sow."

His master replied, "I will judge you by your own words, you wicked servant! You knew, did you, that I am a hard man, taking out what I did not put in, and reaping what I did not sow? Why then didn't you put my money on deposit, so that when I came back, I could have collected it with interest?"

Then he said to those standing by, "Take his mina away from him and give it to the one who has ten minas."

"Sir," they said, "he already has ten!"

He replied, "I tell you that to everyone who has, more will be given, but as for the one who has nothing, even what he has will be taken away. But those enemies of mine who did not want me to be king over them—bring them here and kill them in front of me."

From Jesus' teaching it is clear that we are not to passively sit around and wait for his return. He wanted to challenge the disciples" misconceptions that the kingdom was about to suddenly appear. Rather, the kingdom comes as we use and develop what he has entrusted to us in order to expand and advance his kingdom on earth. In relation to how we connect this advancement through our vocation, Darrow Miller writes:

> God's story reveals that God is the King, the world is his kingdom, and we are his stewards. We are to have dominion over creation. We are to fulfill Christ's mandate to disciple the nations, so that the glory of the nations will be prepared for Christ's return. We are to do this as Christians, not outside the context of our work, and not merely in our work. Our task is to manifest the kingdom of God through our work as part of our calling.[252]

We all have our own unique circles of influence where we can bring God's kingdom. Study the Bible in relation to your work vocation and spheres of influence (see example of a vocational Bible study given in the Appendix).[253] Let's rise up and be the nation builders and reformers in the spheres of society to which God has called us! It is time to return to the forgotten mandate and in whatever areas of society we are called to, work to be catalysts and nation disciplers bringing godly reform and transformation wherever we go.[254]

---

[252] *LifeWork*, 155.
[253] Bible studies relating to vocational callings within the different spheres are available at *www.MondayChurch.org*.
[254] For a more detailed study on what it means to "disciple nations," looking at scripture, history and with modern-day examples and illustrations of those

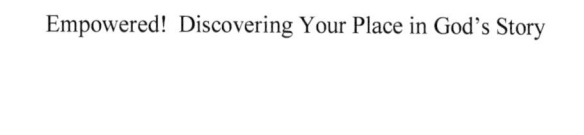

engaged in discipling nations within the different spheres of society, I recommend *His Kingdom Come: An Integrated Approach to Discipling the Nations and Fulfilling the Great Commission* (Seattle: YWAM Publishing, 2008). Other excellent resources are listed at the back of the book.

Part 3

Engaging with Your Story

CHAPTER 9

WHAT ARE *YOU* LIVING FOR?

You see that you are called. You want to engage and live out your story within God's story and mission. But you are not sure what you are called to.

The next three chapters will help you discover your life passion and calling, and give you some tools to enable you to better understand the person God has made you to be and connect your God-given dreams and passions to living out your destiny as part of God's story!

> Living on purpose is the only way to really live. Everything else is just existing.[255]

> "I press on to lay hold of (grasp) and make my own, that for which Christ Jesus, the Messiah, has laid hold of me and made me His own." (Philippians 3:12, Amplified)

The question of purpose and the reason for living has been an issue that humankind since the beginning of time has sought to find an answer to. Here are some popular views today:[256]

- to live one's dreams

---

[255] Rick Warren, *The Purpose Driven Life: What on Earth Am I Here For?* (Zondervan Publishing, 2002), 312.
[256] http://en.wikipedia.org/wiki/Purpose_of_life.

- to become the person you've always wanted to be
- to seek happiness and flourish
- to spend it for something that will outlast it
- to expand one's potential in life
- to leave the world a better place than you found it
- to seek pleasure and avoid pain
- to attain spiritual enlightenment
- to live as long as possible

For Christians who have experienced the joy of new life in Jesus Christ, we can rest in the knowledge that at the end of our lives on earth, we will spend eternity with God and all will be well. There will no longer be any pain, suffering or evil. No sickness, war or death. All wrongs will be put right and everything will be as God originally intended.[257] While this is our future hope, what about our time as God's kingdom representatives on earth now? This key issue is what motivated the apostle Paul to pursue the reason and purpose for which Christ had come into his life and made him his own. It was much more than just obtaining a ticket to heaven. It was to share the joy of restoring God's kingdom purposes in the earth.

I remember meeting a couple who had just retired from their respective areas of employment confide in me that they wanted to know what God had for their lives. It was only now in their mid-60s, prompted by no longer having a job to go to in the morning that the question was

---

[257] See Revelation 21:4–5; Isaiah 2:4; 11:6–9.

being asked: *What on planet earth am I here for?* We don't need to wait until we reach retirement age to ask this crucial question.

Discovering Your Life Purpose

Finding out your life purpose is a journey and a process that can begin anytime. If you have yet to embark on this journey of discovery, it can begin right now.

As a trained life coach I've read a number of self-help books on personal development and discovering your life purpose. The steps are essentially the same: Consider your dreams. Determine your strengths and what you are good at. Aim high. Align with your values. Set some goals and develop a plan of action. Connect with others. Go for it! Stay with the course, don't give up and finish well. Leave a legacy and celebrate your successes. These are all good principles, mostly based on the Bible, and will often lead to successful outcomes. We can learn much from them and I incorporate many of the principles into my coaching and leadership training. However, because by definition self-help books are written from a self-centered viewpoint, they overlook a critical starting-point. What matters most is not what *I* want to do or be, but discovering the purpose *God* has created me for.

> "Focusing on ourselves will never reveal our life's purpose." (Colossians 1:16, The Message)

In Chapter 2 I referred to faulty thinking in relation to missions. When we consider God's plan for our lives, we can be subject to faulty thinking too. I have heard people hesitate in wanting to ask God what he has created them to be, in case he tells them something they don't like. "He might tell me to go to India or to some poor tribe in Africa." The Bible tells us that God is love and his plans for our lives are good and not for evil, to give us a future and a hope.[258] As our creator, he knows us better than we know ourselves and designed a wonderful purpose for our lives before we ever existed. It may well be challenging and take us out of our comfort zones, but we can trust in the fact that our heavenly Father only has good things in store for his children. Most kids love treasure hunts (and you only need to visit a local thrift or charity store to notice that many adults do too). The anticipation of hunting for something and then finding it can be very exciting. What is more thrilling is to realize that God has a purpose for our lives that we are to discover!

Finding our Mission within God's Mission

> You may choose your career, your spouse, your hobbies, and many other parts of your life, but you don't get to choose your purpose.[259]

Some parents tell their children, "You can be anything you want to be." Others say, "You can be anything your strengths allow you to be." The biblical perspective is, "You can be all that God has created you to be!" Not only will we be the most effective and fulfilled

---

[258] Jeremiah 29:11.
[259] Rick Warren, *The Purpose-Driven Life: What on Earth Am I Here For?* (Zondervan Publishing, 2002), 21.

when we live according to our God-given design, as noted in Chapter 1, our life story is to be a part of the story that God is writing. Our mission is to be a part of God's mission purpose. Once we understand this, the vital question becomes, "What is my place in God's story?" We are made to live for something bigger than ourselves which is the kingdom of God. We are to bring and advance God's kingdom on earth.

In Chapter 1 we also saw that there are four key elements to God's story: Creation, Rebellion/Fall, Redemption, and Restoration/Consummation. We are living in the third part of God's story where after Christ's work on the Cross (part 3) and prior to the return of the King (the closing act), we are to work towards extending his kingdom on earth by proclaiming the good news of this kingdom gospel, and teaching and discipling nations in the ways of God. Our lives here on earth can have eternal significance as we live in the light of eternity and invest today in God's kingdom that will know no end and last forever.[260]

Kingdom Vision on a Restored Earth

> "By faith he [Abraham] made his home in the promised land like a stranger in a foreign country; he lived in tents, as did Isaac and Jacob, who were heirs with him of the same promise. For he was looking forward to the city with foundations, whose architect and builder is God." (Hebrews 11:9–10)

---

[260] See Isaiah 9:7.

"For here we have no continuing city, but we seek the one to come." (Hebrews 13:14)

One tool life coaches often use to help people determine vision and set goals is to start with the end in mind. It is called "end visioning." What will the dream or vision look like when it is fulfilled? Once the end point or destination is known, working backwards the steps can be determined to see the vision come to pass. Not only is this a useful planning tool, it also helps people consider the "big picture," the ultimate vision that they want to achieve. Without a clear vision, the path ahead becomes foggy and life itself can become mundane and even meaningless.[261]

In referring back to the three major worldviews highlighted in Chapter 1, it is only biblical theism that sees a purpose in time and history. Animists see time as an endless cycle and are enslaved to the effects of the past, whereas secularists see time as a finite supply which is rapidly running out. Fearing extinction at any moment, secularists are enslaved to the clock and must get all they can. Neither worldview serves as a foundation for true progress and development, which a biblically informed worldview does provide with an appreciation of the past (and the lessons which can be learned from it), the enjoyment of the present, and a hope and reason to build for the future.

The Bible gives us a picture of how God's story in relation to the earth will end and a glimpse of eternity that will follow. Some Christians feel there is little value in developing the earth because they believe the earth will be

---

[261] See Proverbs 29:18.

destroyed. Influenced by teachings related to dispensational and rapture theology, many Christians believe that they will soon vacate the earth, which God will then destroy, and then spend eternity in heaven which is located somewhere else. However, the Bible states that the earth will not be burned up but will be refined and restored to its original state.[262] God's intent is to establish his kingdom on a renewed earth. Just as our bodies will be raised to new life, so the earth will be raised to a new state, transformed and liberated from its present condition and the effects of the curse. Like the passing of a caterpillar and the emergence of a butterfly, so a new earth will emerge into a glorious liberty.

> The purpose of God's saving action is to restore man's dominion on earth . . . Jesus did not come to take our souls to a nonmaterial, eternal heaven; he came to restore the kingdom to us. Saints do go to heaven when they die, but they wait there to return with Christ to rule on this earth; heaven is a waiting room until the great restoration . . . Our future is not to worship God in heaven through eternity but to reign on earth.[263]

> " . . . For you have redeemed us to God by your blood out of every tribe and tongue and people and nation, and have made us kings and priests to our

---

[262] The literal meaning of 2 Peter 3:10 is that the earth and everything in it will be" laid bare" or "found" (Gk *heurethesetai*). This is consistent with Romans 8:19–21 and Matthew 5:5 where Jesus said the meek will inherit the earth (Vishal Mangalwadi, *Truth and Transformation*, Seattle: YWAM Publishing, 2009, 222).
[263] *Truth and Transformation*, 226–227.

God; and WE SHALL REIGN ON THE EARTH."
(Revelation 5:9–10, capitals mine)

When we have a biblically-informed view of our future and that it is vitally connected to our planet, it will impact our vision and how we seek to bring God's kingdom to earth, as it is in heaven. It was this understanding that led Protestant reformer, Martin Luther, to state that "If I knew the world would end tomorrow, I would spend today planting an apple tree."

The Greatest Cause

Our purpose and destiny is connected to God's story and to his kingdom mission. To fulfill our *destiny* is to know the *destin*-ation, what it is we are living for; the cause to which we will invest our lives. In the twenty-first century, we live at a time of many "causes." The younger generation is growing up in a cause-centric world. Causes resonate with them–environmental and social justice causes to name just two. Go Green! Save the Planet! Save the Whale! Stop Human Trafficking! Help Haiti! Support Sudan! Protect Life! There are an endless number of causes that are vying for attention and many of them are good and worthwhile. But there is one that should rise to the top of the list. One cause every believer should embrace as the basis for every other cause. It is THE GREAT CAUSE that Jesus left us with before he left our planet.

This book is about this Great Cause, the Great Commission. Hopefully, this book has helped you to understand better the full scope of what the Great

Commission is about, that along with the preaching of the gospel it must also include the discipling and transformation of nations, bringing God's kingdom to earth in a wholistic way that recognizes no spiritual/secular divide, and as such requires the active involvement of every believer. Greg Stier, founder and president of Dare 2 Share, a ministry committed to mobilizing teenagers to reach their generation for Christ, questions whether use of the term "the Great Commission" is still culturally relevant. He writes,

> Did you know that the term "The Great Commission" is not found in any Bible verse? The phrase began appearing in the 1600s, but it didn't become widely used until the late 18th and early 19th centuries. It first appeared as a section heading in The Scofield Bible in 1907. I'm sure it sounded very hip back then but, hey, so did the King James Version. Thou knowest 'tis true. What's a "great commission"? 20%?
>
> The phrase "The Great Commission" was first popularized by missionaries who used it to infuse interest in evangelism in the hearts of their audiences. They wanted a moniker that would attract people to join Jesus in the greatest mission of all time to tell the greatest story ever told. They hoped that the term would recruit more givers and goers when it came to missions work, especially when it came to young people. They succeeded. The

term was used to recruit thousands upon thousands into foreign missions.

But most teenagers today only associate the word "commission" with sales people. If you refer to "The Great Commission," the typical teenager either scratches his/her head in confusion or tunes you out. Instead of being a ringing call to a grand mission, it's just as likely to stir thoughts of the 20% commission the sales guy at T-Mobile might have just raked in. The term has lost its panache with today's culture. It just doesn't resonate.[264]

It was Hudson Taylor, the English missionary to China and catalyst God used to initiate the Second Wave of missions that popularized use of "the Great Commission" term.[265] We certainly do not need to be bound to it. What is more important is whether we are living its essence. Whether we are living each day and investing our lives into what it seeks to describe . . . the coming of God's kingdom to earth.

Dress Rehearsal for our Eternal Assignments

I find it intriguing to hear about people who want to live a life of purpose without any spiritual basis. Purpose is said to be discovered from the inside, found by enhancing life in some way for others on the planet. While some seek to

---

[264] http://www.dare2share.org/energize/who-else-wants-to-make-evangelism-a-priority-for-teens/(accessed 19 July 2011).
[265] It is believed that Lutheran missionary, Justinian von Welz (1621–1688) coined the term.

deny a source for this purpose outside of themselves, as if to avoid being "enslaved" to the agenda of Another, such a self-generated purpose can only last a lifetime at best. However, a biblical worldview recognizes that life on earth counts for far more than just the time you are here.

Life on earth is just the dress rehearsal before the real production. Just as the nine months inside our mother's womb prepared us for life, so our life here on earth is to prepare us for the next. Our unique God-given assignment here on earth is merely the precursor for what he wants to assign us for eternity. That task will not involve toil, sweat or tears but will be totally satisfying and fulfilling work, just as God originally intended. As C.S. Lewis wrote at the end of the children's fiction series, *The Chronicles of Narnia,* when this world comes to an end, for those in God's kingdom it will just be the beginning of the real story God has planned.

> For us this is the end of all the stories . . . But for them it was only the beginning of the real story. All their life in this world . . . had only been the cover and the title page: now at last they were beginning Chapter One of the Great Story, which no one on earth has read, which goes on forever and in which every chapter is better than the one before.[266]

Man is to participate in and help hasten the completion of God's story outworked in history. As players on the world stage, men and women can be creators of history, working with God to see his purposes fulfilled and

---

[266] C. S. Lewis, *The Last Battle* (Harper Collins, 1956, 1994).

the blessing first spoken to Abraham, extended to all peoples and nations. Rather than trying to determine the timing of Christ's return, we are exhorted to be faithful stewards in advancing his kingdom now on earth by using the gifts, abilities and opportunities that we have received. What we do with the life we have been entrusted with *now* will determine what we do *in eternity*. Not *where* we will spend eternity but *how*. We are not saved *by* our works but we are saved *to* work. Such faithful discharge of one's responsibilities will receive rewards during the eternal rule of a renewed planet earth.[267]

In the previous chapter we considered the Parable of the Talents recorded in Luke 19 and Matthew 25. I would like to return to it and highlight three key elements:

Calling—Jesus called his servants

Equipping—he equipped them with resources for the task

Task/assignment—he gave them the task

In chapters 6 and 8 we considered the calling and the equipping of every believer. We noted that there is a general and particular *call* on every believer's life. We then saw that he wants every believer to be *equipped* for the task that he has for them. This is God's investment in you! The talents in the parable represent the capital or investment that was entrusted to the servants. Capital investment is intended to be put to work and just as in the world of

---

[267] See Matthew 24:45–25:46.

business, God expects a return on his investment. He expects our lives to be fruitful and productive, that the seed of his kingdom in us will expand and be multiplied to be a blessing in the lives of many others. The *task* we have all been given is to be about the Father's business . . . the family business . . . kingdom business. The return on investment God is looking for is the advancement of his kingdom; for the "mustard seeds" of his kingdom to expand and transform the world.[268] Understanding how God has invested in our lives will help us to discover our unique calling. This is the issue to which we now turn.

---

[268] See Jesus' kingdom parable recorded in Matthew 13:31–32, Mark 4:30–32 and Luke 13:18–19.

CHAPTER 10
DISCOVERING YOUR UNIQUE ROLE IN GOD'S KINGDOM MISSION

Our purpose and destiny is connected to God's story and to his kingdom mission. As we live for a cause greater than our own lives—God's Great Cause, the Great Commission—we will seek to channel our abilities, energies and who God has made us for the advancement of God's kingdom.

God has made each one of us for a purpose. Like any designer, before we were created, God designed who we would be. As we look around it is clear that God likes variety as every person who has ever been born is uniquely different. This is a scientific fact of life. The discovery of DNA–our written digital code and genetic language—has shown us an infinite number of ways DNA molecules can come together which means you will never meet someone exactly like you! The Bible says that we are fearfully and wonderfully made,[269] and that we are God's very own workmanship, his creative and original masterpieces.[270] Just as we all have unique fingerprints and DNA, we each have a special role to play on planet earth. No one can fulfill that role for us. It is our divine assignment, our life purpose.

Discovering our life purpose is a process, a journey that continues throughout our lives. As we seek God and

---
[269] Psalm 139:13.
[270] Ephesians 2:10.

take faith steps along the way, he will reveal to us who he has made us to be. He is at work in us both to be willing to do and to carry out his good purpose for our lives.[271] There are some things we can do to help us in our journey of discovery.

Our God-given SHAPE

> God's purpose or intention for our lives is revealed in our design. Just as you can determine the purpose for the eyes or lungs by examining them, so the way we are made and the gifting we have, reveal God's unique purpose for our lives. The word design is related to the word designation, referring to direction or appointment.[272]

Let us now consider our unique design because like any good designer, there is a purpose behind how our own designer, God, has made us. Discovering our design will aid us in recognizing our purpose. Pastor and author, Rick Warren, in his best-selling book, *The Purpose Driven Life*, gives a useful acronym to highlight five key factors: SHAPE.[273]

> **S**piritual gifts
> **H**eart
> **A**bilities

---

[271] Philippians 2:13.
[272] Darrow L. Miller, *My Place in HIStory: Discovering Your Calling* (Disciple Nations Alliance, 2009), 9.
[273] *The Purpose Driven Life: What on Earth Am I Here For?* (Zondervan Publishing, 2002), Days 30–31.

Personality
Experience

Let us consider each one in turn.

Spiritual Gifts

> "But to EACH ONE of us grace was given according to the measure of Christ's gift." (Ephesians 4:7)

> "As EACH ONE has received a gift, minister it to one another, as good stewards of the manifold grace of God." (1 Peter 4:10)

Most Bible scholars classify spiritual gifts into three categories: ministry gifts, motivational gifts, and manifestation gifts. These relate to the three major passages on spiritual gifts, Ephesians 4, Romans 12, and 1 Corinthians 12. Christians have been given these *"charismata"* gifts to serve one another and to build God's kingdom.

Ministry Gifts (Ephesians 4:7–16)
These equipping gifts given by the Son are to facilitate and assist every believer to work out their particular callings and life purpose. They are often illustrated by the five fingers of the hand.

These gifts are often recognized and function within the context of church congregations. However, could it be that these gifts are also given to advance God's kingdom in every other area and sphere of society? With this in mind and to assist those who sense they have a ministry gift but feel that its primary function is outside of the religious sphere, some additional terms have been added.[274]

Apostolic (Entrepreneur, Visionary, Pioneer, Innovator, Strategist, Activist)–take the lead in pioneering or overhauling initiatives that have lost a sense of purpose and direction; may function in many or all of the ministry gifts, likened to the "thumb," the strongest of all fingers, able to touch every finger.

Prophetic (Consultant, Advocate, Troubleshooter, Questioner, Non-conformist, Reformer, Radical)–mouthpiece, points to the future and brings words of correction and challenge in regards to attitudes, behavior, ethics and obedience to the word of God; the index finger, or pointer finger.

Evangelistic (Communicator, Networker, Recruiter, Reconciler)–bringing others into the Body through effectively and frequently communicating the gospel; may use preaching, drama, music and other creative ways; the "middle finger," the longest of the fingers reflecting the fact that this gift reaches out further than the others.

Pastoral (Care-Giver, Guide, Mentor, Nurturer, Humanizer)–called to stay, nurture, guide and care for groups of believers toward significant growth; the "ring finger," the finger of love and marriage.

Teaching (Instructor, Educator, Trainer, Researcher)–a foundational ministry bringing understanding of God's Word, digging into the scriptures

---

[274] Some terms are drawn from M. Frost and A. Hirsch, *The Shaping of Things to Come* (Peabody: Hendrickson, 2003), 175.

and concerned with the details; represented by the smallest finger which is able to get into the tight places and dissect the word of truth.

Manifestation Gifts (1 Corinthians 12:7–11)

The nine manifestation gifts outlined in 1 Corinthians 12 are given by the Holy Spirit to build up the Church and reveal God's presence through utterance, power, and revelation. These gifts are not possessed by people but are supernatural abilities given by the Holy Spirit in moments of need to advance God's kingdom. They are not just intended for use within a church context but as tools to equip us in everyday life for kingdom mission. In the gospel accounts we see a number of them in operation in the life of Jesus as he encountered different people and situations.[275]

Motivational Gifts (Romans 12: 4–8)

These gifts of the Father seem to represent basic *motivations,* usually represented by a "gift mix," rather than one singular gifting. They are a part of who we are and how God has made us. Here is the list given in Romans 12 with some additional words used to help expand on the description of the gifting so as to aid application outside of the church context and across all the spheres of influence within society:

PROPHETIC—Perceivers, Inspirers, Questioners, Non-Conformists and Revolutionaries see things that others don't and speak with boldness and insight, typically

---

[275] For example, the word of knowledge (John 4:17–18), the word of wisdom (Matthew 22:15–21; Mark 12:13–17; Luke 20:20–26), word of prophecy (Matthew 24), along with the many gospel accounts of healings and miracles.

demonstrating moral courage and an uncompromising commitment to worthy values (the "eyes" of the Body)

HELPS/SERVICE—these Helpers, Servers, and Doers have a strong desire to serve others; may fulfill significant responsibilities as a loyal #2 person; take effective action to provide for the practical, physical needs of others (the "hands")

TEACHING/RESEARCHING/EDUCATING/TRAINING—Teachers, Researchers, Educators and Trainers like to provide clear instruction that results in understanding information or truth (the "mind")

GIVING/SHARING/CONTRIBUTING—Givers, Sharers and Contributors respond with wisdom to special needs by giving or investing in people or projects (the "arms")

EXHORTATION/ENCOURAGEMENT—these Exhorters and Encouragers catalyze personal development out of a keen awareness of a person's growth needs (the "mouth")

LEADERSHIP/ADMINISTRATION/FACILITATION/MANAGEMENT—these Leaders, Facilitators, Administrators, Managers and Owners cast vision, enlist others, and coordinate their efforts towards initiatives that fulfill a specific purpose; organize information, people, or resources to more efficiently accomplish goals or purposes (the "head")

MERCY/COMPASSION/KINDNESS—people with the gift of Mercy, Compassion and Kindness suffer with, comfort, and provide hope for those who are in pain (the "heart").

A Spiritual Gift Questionnaire to help you identify your ministry and motivational gifts can be found in the Appendix at the back of the book.

Gift Mix

In practice, individuals will have a spiritual gift mix of ministry and motivational gifts. This cluster of gifts will include dominant gifts supported by other strengths and gifting.

Heart and Passions

In the Bible the word "heart" is used to refer to a person's desires, passions, motivations, interests and dreams. It is what gives us energy and meaning, what we care about, enjoy and love to do. We are exhorted to "serve the Lord with all our heart," not out of a sense of duty or obligation but out of a deep desire and longing. As we live from our heart we will be effective in what we do.

Recognizing your primary Motivational Gift will aid you to function out of who God has made you to be. To help you identify more specifically your heart passions so that these can be directed into your assigned area of deployment and sphere(s) of influence, prayerfully consider your answers to the following questions (you may find it worthwhile to also write down your answers):

- If you could do anything, what would it be?
- What would you do if you knew you could not fail?
- What do you love to talk about the most?

- If money was not an issue, what would you do?
- What energizes you and makes you come alive?
- What would you do and how would you spend your time if you learned today that you only had six months to live?
- Is there an issue that really grieves your heart? (What grieves you is a clue to something you may be assigned to heal/address e.g. abused and molested children? Sex/human trafficking? Ignorance? Disease? Poverty? Debt? Pornography? Abortion?)
- Is there an issue that you hate and get angry about?
- What sphere(s) of society do you have a passion for?
- What interests are you drawn to? (e.g. art, animals, health and nutrition, science, music, business, politics, the environment, those emotionally damaged)
- How can you connect your interests to your sphere(s) of influence and calling?

Abilities and Talents

"He has filled them with skill to do all kinds of work as craftsmen, designers, embroiderers in blue, purple and scarlet yarn and fine linen, and weavers—all of them master craftsmen and designers." (Exodus 35:35)

Our natural abilities and talents are what we were born with and what developed during our formative years growing up as children. Unlike skills which are learned and acquired throughout our lives, abilities are our God-given "hard-wiring" and are clear indicators of what God has called us to.

Have you ever been in some kind of team where you had to take a role that did not suit you? For example, a wrong position in a sports team, being asked to play the guitar when you are really a drummer, being asked to do the accounts when you love to teach? This can be made worse when you see somebody else doing badly the thing you know you are really good at and should have been asked to do! The Bible gives parents the responsibility of helping their children discover and develop their strengths. Proverbs 22:6 exhorts, "Train up a child in the way he should go [and in keeping with his individual gift or bent], and when he is old he will not depart from it."

In recent years it has become popular to identify one's strengths.[276] Research indicates that fewer than a quarter of us actually play to our strengths.

Everything God does is for a purpose and so the natural abilities he has equipped you with are not without reason. God doesn't waste abilities. Find out what you do well and do more of it; find out what you don't do well and stop doing it. As we do so, we will align ourselves with whom God has made us to be and become more effective in what we do.

---

[276] The "Clifton Strengths Finder" (www.strengthsfinder.com) is a web based questionnaire, which based on the answers claims to be able to define 34 individual "strengths".

The *Highlands Ability Battery* is unique among assessment tools because it provides objective measurements of natural abilities. Because it does not depend on self-reporting or on subjective appraisals, it gives you a clear and powerful picture of who you really are. Further details can be found in the Appendix at the back of the book.

As we discover the abilities and talents God has entrusted us with, we should dedicate them to him and for use in his kingdom. The Living in One World diagram in Chapter 6 highlights that our abilities can either be consecrated and used for God, or unconsecrated and used merely for our own ends. History is full of people who were blessed by God with a unique gift and ability but while they may have used them to bring about personal fame and fortune, they did not dedicate them to God for his use. As a result, they have no eternal value.

Once identified, as good stewards of what we have been given we should also seek to develop our talents with appropriate skills.

Personality

Another aspect of how God has wired us is our personality. This is a consistent set of characteristics and tendencies that influence how we think, feel and behave as people. Current research indicates that our personality is a result of both genetic and environmental factors.

Different personalities are suited to different roles and callings in life. There are no "right" or "wrong" temperaments. Jesus chose twelve disciples who expressed different personalities. Similarly, God has made and chosen you with your unique combinations of gifts, abilities and personality, because he loves you and wants to express himself through who you are!

There are various tools and assessments available to help you identify and understand your personality. Some popular personality profiles are referred to in the Appendix.

How can you employ your personality to contribute to his kingdom mission?

Experience

A biblically informed worldview knows that my existence and who I am is not a product of chance or the result of some cosmic accident. I, for instance, was born in England in the mid-1960s of white Anglo-Saxon parentage, into a family with a Protestant Christian heritage going back four generations. I did not have a choice in any of these matters. I did not ask to be English, European or a white male. This is just who I am. There may be things we wish had been different but ultimately we must leave them in the hands of a providential God who is able to turn even what may appear as our disadvantages into advantages and wonderful sources of blessing.

As God's workmanship we have been born for a reason and for a specific purpose, even though it may not be immediately apparent to us right now. Even the circumstances of our birth, our parents and ethnic origin, where we were born and the generation in which we came into the earth, none of these things were accidental. There is a purpose behind them.

Understanding our life history and the phase of life we are currently in can help us recognize how God is working in our lives. In researching the lives of hundreds of Christian leaders, J. Robert Clinton identified six phases which characterize the stages a leader can pass through during the course of his/her life (see Appendix). While Clinton's model was specifically developed in the context of leadership development, I believe it can be helpful for anyone seeking to understand in a general sense God's working in our lives, both in terms of spiritual and character formation, and in the development of his ministry in and through us. In this way we not only consider *who* we are in terms of our gifts, abilities, passions and so on, but also take note of *where* we are in our journey of discovery. An appreciation of this process can help us avoid trying to rush ahead of God and encourage us to persevere during the hard times, knowing that God will accomplish his purposes in and through us as we continue to trust and depend on him.

In addition to our family of origin and other issues which define who we are from birth, there are other life experiences that shape us that often God uses to prepare us for kingdom work and service. Here are seven kinds of experiences that should be examined:

Family experiences—values, modeling, heritage, cultural background?

Educational experiences—favorite subjects and learning, cross-cultural exposure, life experiences? What kind of knowledge did I acquire?

Vocational experiences—effective and enjoyable jobs, training received? What have I done well?

Spiritual experiences—meaningful encounters with God? Seeds of destiny? Life calling scripture verses or prophetic words received?

Ministry experiences—how served God in the past? Where has there been a sense of God's blessing and empowerment?

Painful experiences—problems, hurts, trials?

Relational experiences—friendships, associations, connections, teachers/mentors, role models?

In addition, reflect on significant events and turning points in your life.

How can your experiences help you impact the spheres of life and society where you live and work?

How can your credentials open up opportunities within your sphere(s) of influence or focus area?

How can you network with others of like mind to influence your sphere(s) of influence?

Prayer, Reflection, and Affirmation

As previously mentioned, growing in self-awareness and discovering God's design and purpose for our lives is a process, sometimes a long one. However, God wants to reveal them to you and going through the above areas will assist as you journey with him and take faith steps along the way. As you discover and consider your spiritual gifts, the passions and issues close to your heart, your natural abilities and talents, your personality and your experiences, write down and record the key insights you receive and pray over them. Share what you sense God is revealing to you with a trusted friend. The support and affirmation of others can be very encouraging and sometimes they may recognize something in us that we do not see ourselves!

As you grow in a deeper appreciation of whom God has made you and the desires and motivations in your life, ask God to show you how his investment in your life can best serve his kingdom purposes.

It is worth noting that sometimes God will call us to do something that does not seem to be in line with our natural abilities, gifts, strengths, personality and passions.[277] This is more the exception than the rule although even when we are utilizing our God-given abilities and motivations, we must always ensure that our dependency is not based on our natural talents but is in the power and anointing of God's Spirit within us.

In Chapter 6 when considering the calling of every believer, we noted that all work, provided that it is moral, can be considered "spiritual" and of value to the kingdom of God. The key question is whether we are living a consecrated life or not, one that is set apart and dedicated to God and his kingdom or one that is directed by self-interest? Living in a culture that is highly materialistic provides a constant temptation to evaluate decisions related to career, vocation and what we invest our lives in solely on the basis of salary, status, and job satisfaction. These things

---

[277] Biblical examples would include stuttering Moses being called to be God's mouthpiece before Pharaoh; Jonah, the reluctant missionary being sent to the city of Nineveh; and the apostle Paul who by his own admission was not a powerful speaker but was chosen by God to be an apostle to the Gentile nations.

are not wrong in themselves but we need to honestly ask ourselves what is the primary criteria for doing what I do? Am I living for God's agenda and his kingdom mission or for my own agenda?

Integration and Application

Whatever role God has called us to within his story and mission, we need to understand that it will not happen automatically, just because God has made us and equipped us for a particular task. As the apostle Paul wrote to the believers in Philippi, we have to lay hold of and grasp our destiny in God, making it our own,

> "I press on to lay hold of (grasp) and make my own, that for which Christ Jesus, the Messiah, has laid hold of me and made me His own." (Philippians 3:12, Amplified)

In the Appendix I have included a chart that will help you integrate all the factors that make up your SHAPE and God-given design. You may also wish to ask a Christian life coach, or a leader or friend who is able to help you, to bring all the pieces together so that you can begin to identify and articulate your life direction and purpose.

Calling Statement

One way we can articulate our calling and life purpose is to create a summary statement. This is sometimes referred to as a *Personal Mission Statement*. It may be one or two sentences, or a short paragraph. The most effective statements are ones that are concise, easily understood and easy to remember. This may take some time to develop and formulate, and may need to be reviewed and modified as you journey with God and your purpose and life direction becomes clearer.

> "Write the vision and make it plain on tablets, that he may run who reads it." (Habakkuk 2:2)

You may also like to create a more visual image (sometimes referred to as a *Vision Board*) which not only sets out your Calling or Personal Mission Statement, but also incorporates photographs, pictures, a scripture verse or prophetic words that represent or relate to your calling and life assignment.

Focus Areas

As we discover who God has made us and for what unique purpose, we have established that this is to be worked out within God's purpose and kingdom mission. We have also noted that the Great Commission involves the discipling of nations and bringing the gospel of the kingdom to every sphere of every nation. His kingdom is to be applied in every sphere or domain of society—such as education, government, the family, media, arts and entertainment, business and so on.

Most of us are involved in more than one sphere and we all have different roles in these spheres of influence. For example, we may be a parent of a family, a business owner, and a voluntary worker for a local political party. Some of our involvements represent responsibilities that we have at different phases of life. Others may relate to a particular passion that we have for an area.

The Appendix includes a table listing a range of Focus Areas including different spheres of society along with people groupings within these various domains.

Prayerfully consider and determine what particular sphere of society you have a passion for? It may be helpful for you to review the questions in the section above on identifying your *"heart."* Describe that passion and seek God on how this passion can be used within that sphere to advance his kingdom.

CHAPTER 11
INTENTIONAL ACTION

Once you have discovered your sense of calling and area or sphere of deployment, start to be deliberate in building and advancing the kingdom of God. Just because there are Christian believers present in various spheres of society does not mean that God's kingdom is expanding in those domains. We have to be intentional in using our God-given gifts and abilities to bring kingdom influence and work towards societal transformation. Taking as an example an entrepreneur functioning out of an apostolic gift, Dean Sherman writes,

> There has to be a sense of call from God and an intentional strategy to reach people and to meet the needs of society rather than just expanding the company to a foreign market or being a believer in the marketplace. This purposeful, anointed interface of a full-stature church-building kingdom in society is what we would call discipling nations. We all have irrevocable gifts and callings from God himself. We must encourage one another to seek God and his specific will for our lives. Perhaps this is even part of seeking first his kingdom as opposed to seeking first to feed and clothe ourselves (Matt. 6).[278]

---

[278] Dean Sherman, "The Church and the Kingdom," in *His Kingdom Come: An Integrated Approach to Discipling Nations and Fulfilling the Great Commission* (Seattle: YWAM Publishing, 2008), 177.

Study the Bible in relation to your vocation and calling. For example, seek out what the scriptures have to say about health, business, government, education or whatever it is you are called to and get together with others called to the same domain to discover the biblical principles and mind of Christ in relation to your sphere of influence.[279] An example of a vocation-related Bible study can be found in the Appendix.

In Chapter 4 we noted that at different times throughout history, Christian men and women have engaged in nation discipling activity within various areas of society; individuals such as William Carey, John Wesley, John Calvin, and Elizabeth Fry. On the other hand, others have sought to "disciple" nations in non-biblical ways. In Chapter 4, I highlighted the significant impact of John Dewey's secularist agenda on Western education, but let us consider the changing impact on one of the other major spheres—the family—that has been witnessed in the West over the past one hundred years.

Whereas Protestant Reformer, Martin Luther, shaped the West's ideas of sex and marriage for more than 400 years through his exposition of the biblical view of marriage being monogamous and life-long, during recent decades this has been attacked and eroded on a number of fronts. At the turn of the twentieth century, the influence of

---

[279] *Lifework: Developing a Biblical Theology of Vocation* is a free, downloadable resource that contains a narrative and series of vocation-related Bible studies and exercises that will help you understand a Biblical perspective of vocation and develop a "biblical theology" for your particular vocational area, leading to practical steps you can take to align your faith and work (www.mondaychurch.org/theology). Sphere or domain Bible study references can also be found at www.templateinstitute.org.

psychologist Sigmund Freud's writings on sexual liberation was built upon by individuals such as Playboy founder, Hugh Hefner, along with songwriters, singers and popular music bands such as the Beatles, who then spearheaded the sexual revolution beginning in the 1960s and instigated a more "permissive society" and universal moral breakdown. Instead of love expressed by a commitment for a lifetime between one man and one woman, society has accepted an alternative lifestyle which includes casual "free love" and premarital sex, cohabitation, teen pregnancy, abortion and pornography; the destructive results of which are evident in the rapid rise in divorce, the breakdown of marriage, the normality of "the single parent family," not to mention the harmful affect on the children produced by this way of living. Such a change has occurred gradually, much like Jesus' analogy of yeast permeating a loaf of bread, and has been influenced by people engaging in different spheres of society, including expressions in literature (the arts), the publication of non-fiction sex manuals (education), the development of birth control (science and technology), and explicit sex scenes on the television or movie screen (the media), to name just a few examples. What this highlights in a negative way also serves to illustrate how nations can be influenced and transformed from a biblical worldview, when believers as agents of God's kingdom ways, embrace a biblical worldview and consecrate and use their gifts for his glory.

Present-day Kingdom Agents and Nation Builders

Every believer has a calling to be a kingdom agent and nation builder in whatever spheres of influence God has placed them. Here are some examples of people pursuing their callings and passions within different spheres of society.

    David comes from a family of storytellers and travelers. When he went to film school he knew that his desire to create movies was not just a childhood dream but a deep passion. As a follower of Jesus and now a Hollywood film director, David looks to God for inspiration and direction as he seeks to use filmmaking as a powerful medium of communication and culture formation to make a kingdom difference in a hurting world.

    Michelle grew up enjoying animals and nature. However, as a missionary in Asia she never imagined that she could combine these interests with missions. She wasn't sure God would approve . . . wasn't missions about preaching the gospel, providing medical care, starting churches and Bible translation? Once Michelle began to realize that the gospel of the kingdom is broader than these activities and that God is honored and glorified when we are the people he has made us to be, she felt empowered to use animal-assisted therapy to reach out to the hurting, bruised and emotionally deprived or traumatized. After working with orphaned children in Thailand, Michelle is planning to use her therapy dog to minister to emotionally traumatized children in a western nation, bringing healing, building trust, and being a part of breaking the negative cycle of divorce and creating a positive future for these children.

Although Julia came from a multiple-divorce family, after becoming a Christian, marrying and having her own family she was determined that she would give her children the best possible start in life by modeling a godly marriage, and investing in their lives through building a solid spiritual foundation from the Word of God. It wasn't always easy to lay aside the development of her own gifts in order to focus on the daily investment required, not only in the physical demands of caring for her children but also with the personal daily discipline required to teach the children at home. However, it was also rewarding to talk about and involve God very naturally when studying subjects such as science and history, having devotional times around the table, and dealing with sibling conflicts and the various character forming challenges which are the part of every family's life. Julia believes the most formative part of her children's education was spending quality time with them, allowing them to see and be a part of her husband's and her own relationship with God and how this shaped everything they did as a family. With lots of prayer and by God's grace, investing in the next generation became a priceless venture yielding rich rewards, advancing God's kingdom through godly offspring. Julia's children all love God and are now using their gifts to make a kingdom difference in the world.

With a passion for outdoor activities and for bringing a godly influence in her community, Anne's Norwegian company, NorTrex runs skis schools in the winter and offers a variety of day trips and adventure experiences during the summer high season. Through the business, Anne sees her job and that of her staff as revealing and showing the attributes of God by affirming and enjoying the goodness of creation to the people who come with them on a glacier, kayak or caving trip. She is also intentional about modeling kingdom values such as having an attitude of service, dealing with integrity, and working with excellence and skillfulness. In addition, NorTrex seeks to be an agent of transformation in the local community by providing internships and training to help create jobs and opportunities for young people, and empowering them by helping them develop their skills and character. In this way, Anne's company is helping to address the social problems associated with young people moving out of local communities into the bigger cities. Having gained influence and respect within her community, Anne has been asked by other business leaders and officials to input into other ways that make the area attractive for youth and students to live and work.[280]

On his farm in Virginia, Joel raises livestock using wholistic methods of animal husbandry, free of potentially harmful chemicals. While conventional agriculture is trying to make agriculture a factory or a physical system, Joel has created a model that can save the family farm where people don't have to have thousands of acres and huge amounts of debt. Joel says he is just copying creation and using God's design as a template in raising animals and stewarding the land. His philosophy of farming, which he considers his ministry, emphasizes healthy grass on which animals can

---

[280] Adapted from the article, Extreme Business! Kayaking and the Kingdom in Norway (http://www.businessasmission.com/76.html).

thrive in a symbiotic cycle of feeding. Cows are moved from one pasture to another rather than being centrally corn fed. Then chickens in portable coops are moved in behind them, where they dig through the cow dung to eat protein-rich fly larvae while further fertilizing the field with their droppings. As a result high quality "beyond organic" meats are produced which are raised using environmentally responsible, ecologically beneficial, sustainable agriculture. Joel's pioneering and innovative techniques are described by admiring colleagues and competitors as above reproach and have resulted in Joel now spending a hundred days a year lecturing at colleges and to environmental groups.[281]

Stefan is an artist from India and after several years working with a Christian relief and development agency, he became increasingly excited about the idea of artists being disciplers of nations. Stefan's work is a surrealist response to a very real world and he finds his art returning inexorably to topics of social justice and the marginalized. In his desire to connect art to questions of human dignity, Stefan moved into a full-time art career. Opening a gallery in Delhi with a vision to impact society with beauty and truth, Stefan also runs a residency program for Indian and international artists, and seeks to create opportunities for the marginalized to make art and find a voice. Stefan's personal style juxtaposes imagery to create emotional tensions and bridges that provoke thought.[282]

---

[281] From articles The Good Shepherds by Rob Moll (http://www.christianitytoday.com/ct/2007/october/43.64.html) and High Priest of the Pasture by Todd S. Purdum (http://query.nytimes.com/gst/fullpage.html?res=9D0CE7DF173EF932A35756C0A9639C8B63&pagewanted=1).
[282] http://www.limnersociety.com/people.php#/Limners (accessed 26 August 2011).

Bob is a highly influential attorney whose deep passion for justice led him to create Restore International, a nonprofit organization that endeavors to address atrocities and injustices throughout the world. With a passion and vision for finding audacious ways to restore justice to children and the poorest of the poor, Bob's mission is to speak on behalf of those who do not otherwise have a voice.[283]

Grassroots News International (GNI) is a web-based initiative with the goal of reaching people with honest stories from around the world and using creative multimedia to be advocates for love, hope and change. Students, volunteers and people from all walks of life are joining together to see something unprecedented: an honest look at our world from a grassroots perspective. When much of the international press was still days away from the heartbreak and heroes of the epicenter of the Haitian earthquake, Grassroots news reporters from within the community were already on the scene. When sex slavery went unnoticed on the streets of America, their cameras exposed the injustice.[284]

Bengal Creative Media is a contemporary company of artists who are using the creative arts to address critical issues in Bengali society. They do live performances in cities and villages throughout Bangladesh. Drama is a favorite form of both entertainment and instruction in low literate Bengali society. These gifted artists have a Creative Arts Center where they train people in theater development, music, song, and dance. They produce videos to be

---

[283] http://2011.jubileeconference.com/bob-goff/(accessed (19 August 2011).
[284] www.grassrootsnews.tv.

distributed widely in Bengali society. Their work deals with critical issues facing the society, using biblical wisdom to address these issues. Some of the issues they address are abortion, polygamy, dowry, corruption, health care, illiteracy, child rights, and godly living. God is using this group of Christians to bring Beauty and Truth into this very needy culture.[285]

The Christian Leadership Network (CLN) is a group comprising some 80 church leaders who represent virtually every denomination in the city of Toowoomba, Australia. Together they seek to be the "city church" representing Christ and his kingdom to Toowoomba. One initiative CLN has started is called City Women which aims to make their city a better place for women and girls. For example, Bella Generation encompasses a number of City Women initiatives that seek to restore dignity and raise a beautiful generation of girls who understand their true value, appreciate their true beauty and live a life of purpose. A line of clothing called Bella G Fashion aims to give young women a funky and eco-friendly positive alternative fashion that highlights their beauty while retaining their dignity. Another initiative, called Collective Shout, campaigns to reduce pornography and challenges corporations, advertisers, and media outlets which objectify women and sexualize girls for marketing purposes.[286]

As every believer discovers who God has made them to be, that they have been called and assigned a life

---

[285] Darrow L. Miller, *Worldview and Art: A Call for Balladeers*, July 2003, 26–27 (http://www.disciplenations.org/uploads/vt/B-/vtB-gpk-2V0_zZU98IUvNw/Worldview-and-Art.NARRATIVE.pdf Accessed 8 August 2011).
[286] http://disciplenations.wordpress.com/2011/08/18/toowoomba-churches-together-transforming-a-city/#respond.

purpose within God's overarching story and mission, and as a result engage in kingdom mission activity within their spheres of influence, the seeds of the kingdom of God will expand and multiply, the yeast of the kingdom will permeate every area of life and the light of truth, goodness and beauty will shine forth in the darkness.

    The will and mission of the Father will be carried out.

    His kingdom will come on earth as it is in heaven.

CONCLUSION

It is no accident that we are alive at this time in the history of the world. These are exciting days to be a part of all that God is doing in the earth. As what some are calling the Fourth Wave continues to emerge and develop, his desire is for us to be participators and not merely spectators, to be the people we were created to be and to fulfill the unique life assignment that we have been entrusted with as part of his story and mission. As believers are affirmed and validated in their callings, equipped, commissioned and released into kingdom work and ministry in all spheres of society, the future holds great expectation for us all. While we will not see the fullness of God's kingdom on earth until Jesus returns, we can be proactive in advancing his reign and ways in the knowledge that we are investing our lives into a kingdom that will know no end. In doing so we need to seek God to understand how the ways of his kingdom can be expressed in all areas of life. This book has sought to highlight the grand scope of God's story, how every believer's story fits within the BIG story, along with providing some practical tools in order to engage with it.

Using the context of the emerging Fourth Wave, here is a summary of the key characteristics as we work towards the climax to God's story and the completion of the Great Commission:

All Believers to . . .

Be engaged. Unlike previous waves which emphasized the "special few" and were primarily driven by the West, the Fourth Wave will be characterized by the whole body of Christ, across the generations and across the cultures, having a missional mindset and being actively engaged. No-one need be excluded. Whereas mission has traditionally been an activity of the church, there is a growing awareness that Christians intentionally engaged in every area of life will increasingly influence society with the kingdom of God.

Be empowered. Effective ministry is about being who we are and what we are called to do, not just within the confines of church meetings or "out there" on the so-called "mission field," but in the home, workplace, and other locations where we spend most of our time. In order for every believer to "find their place," the old division between what is secular and what is sacred must be torn down, along with the limited perspective on the need for people to become "full-time missionaries" by leaving their jobs, and of businesspeople solely being mission "funders." Churches will intentionally release and empower their members, and all countries will become "sending nations," supplying workers to advance the kingdom of God.

Be united. The Fourth Wave will see an unprecedented unity of the Spirit across all expressions of Christ's body for the purpose of seeing God's agenda fulfilled and the prayer of Jesus in John 17 answered. This, in turn, will release the fullness of the blessing of God

(Psalm 133) and the "growth of the Body for the edifying of itself in love" (Ephesians 4:16).

All People in . . .

Every 4K zone and segment of society. All remaining unreached people groups, not just ethnic groupings, but also all segments of society will be engaged, along with post-Christian cultures in the Western world.

All Spheres

Return to a biblically informed kingdom worldview. Great Commission engagement will demonstrate the gospel of the kingdom and require the application of biblical truth to societal ills and in every area of life.

Reawakening of the discipling nations mandate. This focus has been present in previous waves but the Fourth Wave will bring a release of every member of the body of Christ to be intentionally and actively engaged in permeating every sphere of life and society with the ways of God, recognizing that God's redemptive purpose is for nations and the whole of creation, not just for the redemption of humankind.

Innovative ideas. All available technology and resources will be utilized; thinking "out-of-the-box" without being stuck in traditional models and mindsets will be encouraged; and creative communications with a greater use of the arts and media will be adopted in order to reach, teach and immerse whole cultures with the gospel of the kingdom.

The God Factor

Clearly, any new move of God has to be fueled and energized by the breath of God and the wind of the Holy Spirit. In spite of our best efforts, lasting and effective godly transformation will only come about by the hand of God. However, God's people do have to be willing to cooperate with what God wants to do in the earth and be actively engaged in bringing it about.

The Holy Spirit is the active agent of mission. Like the pillar of smoke by night and the cloud by day that led the nation of Israel, the Holy Spirit will always go before the church in its missionary journey. As we seek to find out where and how God is at work we become missional people. What God plans to do in the Fourth Wave will be a work that will not come forth from the plans of man. In many ways it will seem unmanageable and will include many surprises. It will require a total reliance and dependency on the Spirit of God.

In the New Testament we see the Holy Spirit directed God's missionary activity:

> God's missionary Son, Jesus, was conceived by the Spirit, anointed at his baptism by the Spirit, led by the Spirit into the wilderness to overcome Satan, and empowered by the Spirit to begin his kingdom ministry[287]

---

[287] Luke 1:35; 3:21–22; 4:1, 14, 18.

The first disciples were told to wait until they were empowered by the Holy Spirit to be witnesses to God's continuing mission[288]

The Holy Spirit brings about a meeting of Philip with the finance minister of Ethiopia[289]

The Holy Spirit prepares Ananias to receive arch-persecutor Saul[290]

The Holy Spirit prepares Peter to break free of his cherished principles and go to be the guest of a pagan army officer[291]

The Holy Spirit initiates the missionary sending of Paul and Barnabas to the Gentiles[292]

The Holy Spirit guides Paul and Barnabas in their journeys.[293]

God's mission changes not only the world but also the church. Jesus said that the Holy Spirit would not only convict the world, he would also lead the church towards a full understanding of the truth.[294] We see this evidenced in Acts 10 where the Holy Spirit worked to not only bring about the conversion of the Gentile Cornelius, but also a

---

[288] Acts 1:8.
[289] Acts 8:26–40.
[290] Acts 9:10–19.
[291] Acts 10:1–20.
[292] Acts 13:1–2.
[293] For example, Acts 16:7.
[294] John 16:8–15.

conversion in the thinking of the church towards non-Jewish peoples.

While the Holy Spirit is the divine orchestrator and power behind God's dealings in the earth, as God's people we also have a vital role in cooperating with the mission of God. Kingdom transformation starts on the individual level with the renewing and reforming of our minds to a true biblical worldview.

In looking back through mission history, beginning with the birth of the church in the book of Acts, Ron Boehme draws out the key elements that are present in each of the preceding waves which led to a new surge of missionary outreach to take place:[295]

Revival fires—personal hunger for God and supernatural empowerment, e.g. Day of Pentecost, Moravian, Great Evangelical Awakening, Pentecostal and Charismatic Renewals and other outpourings of God's Spirit[296]

Prayer movements—fervent communication with God, e.g. Day of Pentecost, Moravian 24-hour prayer watch, Concerts of Prayer, Haystack prayer meeting, national intercessory groups, national days of prayer,

---

[295] Ron Boehme, 2011.
[296] According to revivalist, Cindy Jacobs, as important and life-transforming as revival is, it is not enough as with the passing of time the influence of society and culture moves back in and everything starts to look as it did pre-revival (from the introduction to her book entitled, *The Reformation Manifesto: Your Part in God's Plan to Change Nations Today*).

Korean prayer mountain, 24/7 prayer, Global Day of Prayer[297]

Unity among believers—love of God taking precedence over differences, e.g. united World Missions conferences, Edinburgh 1910, Lausanne congress, March for Jesus, city-wide church gatherings, AD2000, Call2All.[298]

These three elements will also prepare the way for the Fourth Wave and are the necessary ingredients for any significant move of God. When God's people act, he will move!

Spiritual Warfare

> We live in two worlds—or better, in one world with two parts, one part that we can see and one part that we cannot. We are urged, for our own welfare, to act as though the unseen world (the rest of reality) is, in fact, more weighty and more real and more dangerous than the part of reality we can see . . . things are not what they seem. There is more going on here than meets the eye. Far more.[299]

---

[297] The International Prayer Connect (IPC) links hundreds of prayer networks and ministries to focus on prayer on common global concerns.

[298] Call2All represents a partnership of hundreds of the top missions agencies, denominations, and organizations in the world, including tens of thousands of Christian leaders, with Call2All strategy congresses being held in major cities throughout the world (www.call2all.org).

[299] John Eldredge, *Waking the Dead: The Glory of a Heart Fully Alive* (Thomas Nelson Publishers, 2003), 29.

As we seek to advance the kingdom of God in the earth we must be mindful that we will be engaging in spiritual warfare. The Bible makes clear that a conflict is taking place between God's kingdom and the kingdom of Satan, between the kingdom of light and kingdom of darkness, between good and evil, truth and falsehood, life and death. This is not a battle involving natural weapons such as guns, bombs or swords. Nor is it a fight with other people. It is essentially a spiritual battle engaging with spiritual forces.

> "For we do not wrestle against flesh and blood, but against principalities, against powers, against the rulers of the darkness of this age, against spiritual hosts of wickedness in the heavenly places."
> (Ephesians 6:12)

When God's kingdom advances, Satan will always seek to counter-attack. Unable to hinder the great impact of the First Wave which took the gospel to the coastlands, he sought to undermine the second which sought to penetrate the inland regions with the gospel. As Hudson Taylor was beginning the China Inland Mission, another Englishman, Charles Darwin, was promulgating evolutionary doctrines in the *Origin of Species*. This also led to destructive higher criticism of the Bible and a few years after the first World Missionary Conference in Edinburgh (1910), the first of two world wars, followed by the great worldwide economic depression of the 1930s.[300] Now, with the emergence of the Fourth Wave and a growing return to the missional calling of the church, we are already seeing an increase in economic, political and environmental turmoil as Satan seeks to avert and hinder what will be an unprecedented move of God across the earth.

As we engage in this battle in the invisible realm we must be assured that Christ Jesus has already gained the victory. We are not vying for a position of victory but are enforcing the victory Jesus Christ has already obtained through his death and resurrection. Jesus declared that he was building his church and the gates of hell would not prevail against it. The church is not to be in a defensive mode, retreating from the spheres of life and society, waiting for Jesus to return and get her out of the world's mess. Rather, the church is to be on the offence, knowing that God's kingdom will prevail in the end at the consummation of all time.

> "For unto us a Child is born, unto us a Son is given; and the government will be upon His shoulder. And His name will be called Wonderful, Counselor, Mighty God, Everlasting Father, Prince of Peace. Of the increase of His government and peace there will be no end, upon the throne of David and over His kingdom, to order it and establish it with judgment and justice from that time forward, even forever." (Isaiah 9:6–7)

---

[300] C. Gordon Olson, *What in the World is God Doing? The Essentials of Global Missions: An Introductory Guide* (Global Gospel Publishers, 2001), chapter 10.

"Then the seventh angel sounded: And there were loud voices in heaven, saying, "The kingdoms of this world have become the kingdoms of our Lord and of His Christ, and He shall reign forever and ever!" (Revelation 11:15)

As we have already noted, sadly, some Christians have mistakenly believed "the gates of hell" to be synonymous with "the gates of the city," or the spheres of society. As a result, they have either been antagonistic against the domains of government, science or the media, or sought to separate themselves from them altogether. Darrow Miller writes,

> We attack the gates of hell not by lashing out in frustration by ineffective action, nor by closeting ourselves away, but by manifesting more of the culture of the kingdom in the city gates. On the strength of Jesus' word, his church is to take the initiative. It is to take the offense. Because Jesus has said so, truth will challenge the lie, good will overcome evil, love will overcome hate, and light will overcome darkness.[301]

So how do we, as Christians, engage in this warfare that we are involved in? We cannot seek to address every injustice or evil that we are aware of. However, by discovering our unique gifts and calling that we have been entrusted with, we can bring our godly influence into the spheres and areas of life where we have a voice, until the

---

[301] *LifeWork*, Miller, 307–308.

kingdom comes in greater measure and his will is done on earth as it is in heaven.

> There are battles that need to be fought on many fronts. There is a battle for truth and against lies, for the culture of life and against the culture of death; another for justice and against corruption; another for beauty and against the mundane and hideous; another for plenty and against hunger; another for economic sufficiency and against poverty; another for wisdom and against ignorance; and another for health and against disease. Servants of the King are to occupy themselves—using their natural gifts, talents, and abilities—to fight these battles. They are to make a unique contribution, in their life and vocation, to occupy enemy territory for Christ.[302]

God's Mission, Our Mission

In this book we have seen that from the beginning of time God has had a story. In the outworking of history, God has also had a mission. Having created humankind in his image and given them the task of ruling and stewarding the earth and the rest of creation on his behalf, he expressed his desire to enjoy a wonderful relationship with them. Due to man's disobedience, God's mission plan also included a way through his son, Jesus Christ, to redeem sinful man back into a right relationship with his creator. Now, his redeemed people are once again able to fill the earth with the knowledge of God's glory. This becomes the vital task

---

[302] Ibid, 305–306.

of every believer, to be a witness of what they have seen and heard, of what they know to be true, of what they have experienced. God's mission to fill the earth with himself becomes man's mission, our mission.

In more recent history and through three missionary waves, God's glory has swept up to the coastlands, into the inland regions, and made its way to people hidden behind social and cultural barriers. Now, as the momentum continues to build towards the climax of his story, God is initiating a new wave—the Fourth Wave—which will cover and fill the whole earth. This wave will require the intentional and active involvement of every believer making their contribution to demonstrating and bringing God's will and his kingdom to earth. As this is done, God's glorious presence will fill the earth.

The Old Testament provides a wonderful picture of God's presence coming to earth through the building of the tabernacle and temple. God had a detailed plan and called and empowered different ones to use their gifts and abilities to complete the task.[303]

> The variety of occupations used in the building of the tabernacle and temple is astounding: lumbermen, carpenters, spinners, dyers, weavers, embroiderers, seamstresses, foundry workers and metallurgists, goldsmiths, engravers, jewelers, tanners, perfumers, quarry workers, and stone masons. Then there were those who provided direct logistical support: tool makers, keepers of draft animals, seafarers, and laborers . . . There were

---

[303] See Exodus 31:1–6; 35:30–36:2.

those who were involved in the worship activities after the sanctuaries were completed: priests and attendants, musicians, singers, musical instrument makers, and psalmists.[304]

A major thrust of this book has been to demonstrate that every believer has a unique role and contribution to make towards the fulfillment of the Great Commission. In understanding the breadth of this Great Commission mandate, which includes the discipling and teaching of nations, every believer can be empowered and commissioned to use their God-given gifts and abilities in their spheres of influence so that every sphere and domain in society, and every people and culture in the world, can be redeemed back to God.

In what sphere or domain do you believe you are gifted?[305]

In which spheres of society has God given you influence?

The Bible makes clear that Jesus will one day return. He will not only return for his people, his bride the church, but he will also come with rewards for those who have carried out the will of the Father. His message to his disciples was "Occupy till I come," "Do kingdom-business

---

[304] David Bruce Hegeman, *Plowing In Hope: Toward a Biblical Theology of Culture* (Canon Press, 1999), 52.

[305] Through life coaching and the use of assessments designed to help identify natural abilities and personality preferences, the author helps individuals and teams to discover who they are and to be effective in what they do (*www.stuartmsimpson.com*).

until I return."[306] "Bring the kingdom of heaven down to earth."[307]

When the King returns for his kingdom, will he find us engaged in his kingdom work, in whatever spheres of life we are involved in? Our story fits into God's bigger story. Our mission and purpose in life, fits within his global mission and purpose. God is calling us today towards the consummation of his story and his mission. We can help hasten their completion.[308] Discover who you really are and the gifts that he has entrusted to you. Don't stand idle[309] feeling disempowered by dualistic thinking and the lies of the enemy who would have you believe your life is insignificant. Be empowered and be a part of all that God is about to release in the earth. The Fourth Wave is coming. Are *you* going to ride it?

---

[306] Luke 19:13.
[307] Matthew 6:10.
[308] 2 Peter 3:12.
[309] Matthew 20:3.

APPENDIX:
TOOLS TO HELP YOU UNDERSTAND HOW GOD HAS MADE YOU

Contents

Spiritual Gifts Questionnaire

Abilities

Personality Assessments

Life Phase

Focus Areas

Integration–Personal Profile

Vocational Bible Study

Spiritual Gifts Questionnaire[310]

On the questionnaire score yourself 0 to 3, indicating to what extent the statement is true in your life. Do not look at or write on the 'Score Sheet' until after completing the questionnaire.

Much = 3, Some = 2, Little = 1, Not at all = 0

1. I often speak in ways that upset the traditions of people.
2. I enjoy taking responsibility for the well-being of people.
3. I could effectively teach my areas of interest to others.
4. I like to encourage the wavering, troubled or the discouraged.
5. I desire to manage money well in order to give liberally to worthy causes.
6. I enjoy assisting leaders and those in charge so that they can focus on their essential tasks.
7. I have a desire to work with the disadvantaged in order to help give them dignity and alleviate their suffering.
8. I like to persuade others to believe in what I think is important.

---

[310] This Spiritual Gifts Questionnaire has incorporated some question ideas from the Modified Houts Questionnaire published by the Fuller Evangelistic Association and adapted by Barry Austin, as used in the YWAM Leadership Development Course compiled by Stephen Mayers, version 2006. However, in order to not limit the gifts solely to a Church context, some questions have been adapted while others are new to incorporate the broader definitions.

9. I would enjoy carrying the responsibility of leading a group of people to achieve an important purpose.

10. I enjoy breaking new ground with different ways of doing things.

11. When problems need to be resolved I tend to see the issues in terms of black or white and right or wrong.

12. I have enjoyed relating to the same group of people over a long period of time, in their successes and failures.

13. I feel I can explain most things I know something about.

14. I feel I could help stir the complacent and encourage the discouraged to face their challenges.

15. I get a thrill out of giving things or money to initiatives I believe in.

16. I am satisfied just by knowing that my contribution has helped make an event go well.

17. I have felt an unusual compassion for those with physical, emotional or spiritual needs.

18. I can communicate in ways that are engaging and meaningful to the hearers.

19. I can organize ideas, people, resources and time for effective outcomes.

20. I feel I could begin in a pioneering situation and see new initiatives established.

21. Some people really appreciate my insights while others view me as a threat to the status quo.

22. I tend to know those I serve and guide intimately, and to be known well by them.

23. I enjoy devoting a lot of time researching and learning new material to communicate to others.

24. I find that people are often encouraged when I communicate with them and they feel a new lease of life.

25. I feel deeply challenged when confronted with urgent financial needs for causes I believe in.

26. I have enjoyed doing routine tasks that released others to be able to function effectively in what they do best.

27. I would enjoy visiting people in hospitals and/or retirement homes.

28. When I communicate I see a positive effect on the listeners.

29. I am a good judge of when to delegate responsibilities and to whom.

30. I find other people are excited and inspired to follow my vision.

31. If there is compromise within a group or hypocrisy, I am usually one of the first to discern it.

32. I have helped needy people by guiding them to words of hope and comfort.

33. I feel I can instruct others and see resulting changes in knowledge, attitudes, values and conduct.

34. I have inspired people to launch out in faith in an area.

35. I always like to give something if I meet beggars on the street.

36. I don't really mind when others get the credit for what I do.

37. I don't find it difficult to really empathize with and help people who are hurting.

38. I enjoy sharing with people in order to bring about reconciliation and a greater sense of well-being.

39. When a leader shares his/her vision for a group to which I belong, I immediately start thinking of all the things that need to be done in order to achieve the vision.

40. I have a strong desire to start projects in new areas.

41. I am able to perceive and warn against future dangers that most people are not even aware of.

42. I feel I am able to help restore people who have lost their way.

43. I like to equip and train people to be more effective in what they do.

44. I have comforted people in their difficulties in such a way that they felt helped and given fresh hope.

45. I live by the maxim that it is more blessed to give than to receive.

46. I don't need to be in the limelight but I like making everything run smoothly.

47. I would enjoy offering cheerful conversation to a lonely shut-in person, someone in prison, or somebody living on the streets.

48. I feel grieved when I see hopelessness in people and I feel compelled to do something about it.

49. I am able to coordinate the activities of a group of people so that their different gifting complements each other and they function as a unified team.

50. I would enjoy being sent to start something that has never been done before.

Scoring your Spiritual Gifts Questionnaire

Total your scores horizontally on the score sheet.

Place 1, 2, 3 up to 6 in the "My Gifts" column of the highest scoring gifts. This will highlight your "gift mix" combining both ministry and motivational gifts. The first three are your primary gifts. Gifts 4 to 6 are your secondary gifts.

Spiritual Gifts Score Sheet

Value of Answers					Total	My Gifts	Gifts
1	11	21	31	41			Prophetic/Perceiver Reformer/Non-conformist
2	12	22	32	42			Pastoral/Care-Giver/Guide/ Mentor/Nurturer/Humanizer
3	13	23	33	43			Teaching/Instructor/Educator Trainer/Researcher
4	14	24	34	44			Exhortation/ Encourager
5	15	25	35	45			Giving/Sharing/ Contributor
6	16	26	36	46			Helpers/Servers/ Doers
7	17	27	37	47			Mercy/Compassion/ Kindness
8	18	28	38	48			Evangelistic/Communicator/ Networker/Recruiter/Reconc
9	19	29	39	49			Leadership/Administration/ Facilitation/Management
10	20	30	40	50			Apostolic/Visionary/ Entrepreneurial/Pioneer

Abilities

Highlands Ability Battery

The Highlands Ability Battery is an *objective* assessment of your natural abilities and consists of 19 work samples. It's extensive, taking around three hours (but you don't need to complete it in one session) and the results will help you to really understand yourself. It is available online and also on CD.

This is not a "test" in the traditional sense of the word. You can't pass or fail the Highlands Ability Battery! You are asked to do something in each work-sample. How easily you complete a work-sample defines how "naturally" the underlying aptitude comes to you. Each work-sample is timed to reflect your innate abilities and not your skills. A high score isn't better than a low score, it depends on whether a job requires it or not. A low score simply highlights a different kind of ability.

The Highlands Ability Battery was originally developed within industry about 80 years ago. It is psychometrically valid and reliable. This means the information and suggestions that it makes are highly accurate. Compared to the self-assessments that some people use, it is light years ahead and has been described as the equivalent of getting a CAT scan for a painful injury instead of a traditional x-ray.

After you complete the Battery, you receive a 30+ page report describing your results. The report is divided into driving abilities, specialized abilities and personal style. In a 2-hour feedback session (which normally takes place by phone or via Skype, unless face-to-face is possible), a certified Highlands Consultant will go over the results with you and discuss your abilities as they relate to your career and the work roles for which your ability profile ideally suits you.

More information can be found on my Empower Coaching website: *www.stuartmsimpson.com*.

Personality Assessments

A number of questionnaires identify personality based on the four basic temperaments described by the Greek philosopher, Hippocrates: Sanguine, Choleric, Melancholy, and Phlegmatic. In more recent years, these four categories have been given different names but parallel the original distinctions. One example is the **DISC** system which is a very simple self-assessment based on an acronym represented by the four letters:

D—Dominant/Driver (Choleric)–people who are typically forceful, direct, like to take charge, enjoys challenges; seek control

I—Influencing/Inspiring (Sanguine)–people who are typically optimistic, motivational, friendly and talkative; seek recognition

S—Steady/Supporter (Phlegmatic)–people who are typically steady, patient, loyal, cooperative and practical, good team player; seek acceptance

C—Conscientious/Implementer (Melancholic)–people who are typically precise, sensitive and analytical; seek accuracy.

Other more comprehensive systems for identifying personality are the **Myers-Briggs Type Indicator (MBTI)** and the **Enneagram**. The MBTI measures preferences with 16 personality types across 4 scales related to:

1. Where you prefer to get and focus your energy or attention *(Introversion/Extraversion)*

2. What kind of information you prefer to gather and trust *(Sensing/Intuition)*

3. What process you prefer to use in making decisions *(Thinking/Feeling)*

4. How you prefer to deal with the world around you, your "lifestyle" *(Judging/Perceiving)*

Further details on the DISC and MBTI can be found at my coaching website.[311]

Of all the different personality assessments, the Enneagram is my favorite.

The Enneagram

This model defines nine personality types, indicated by the points of a geometric figure (called an *enneagram* from the Greek words *ennea* [nine] and *grammos* [line drawing]). One type is a dominant personality type, complemented by another "wing" element which makes up a second-side to your personality. It also indicates some of the connections between the types.[312]

> *Type description*
> Type One   The Reformer, Perfectionist
> Making things right in the world

---

[311] *www.stuartsimpson.me.*
[312] Christian applications of this human personality model can be explored in *The Enneagram: A Christian Perspective* by Richard Rohr and Andreas Ebert (Crossroads Publishing, 2001) and *Head versus Heart and our Gut Reactions: The 21st Century Enneagram* by Michael Hampton (O Books Publishing), 2005.

Type Two   The Helper, Giver
The needs and wants of others

Type Three   The Achiever, Motivator
Succeeding by getting things done

Type Four   The Individualist, Romantic
Being special and unique

Type Five   The Investigator, Observer
Learning all there is to know

Type Six   The Loyal Skeptic, Questioner
Being the devil's advocate

Type Seven   The Enthusiast, Adventurer
Enjoying and experiencing life

Type Eight   The Challenger, Protector
Being strong and in control

Type Nine   The Peacemaker, Mediator
Maintaining peace and harmony

An online Enneagram Personality Test profiler (questionnaire format) can be found at *www.leadershipwithknowledge.com* or *www.enneagramworldwide.com* (paragraph-based and scientifically validated format).

```
                    The Peacemaker
                         9
    The Challenger 8         1 The Reformer

    The Enthusiast 7         2 The Helper

      The Loyalist 6         3 The Achiever

       The Investigator 5   4 The Individualist
```

[313]

---

[313] Copyright 2013 The Enneagram Institute. All Rights Reserved. Used with Permission.

Life Phase

Your life can be represented by a time line divided into six phases. Though not true for everyone it does provide a functional framework which can be helpful to see how God often works in our lives.[314]

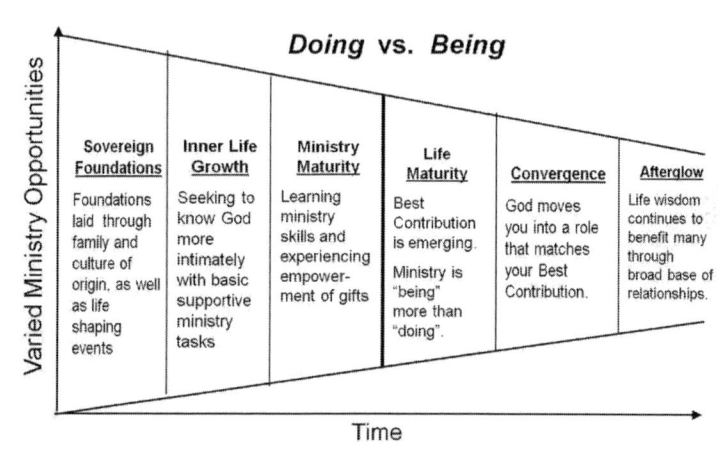

Doing vs. Being

Varied Ministry Opportunities

Sovereign Foundations	Inner Life Growth	Ministry Maturity	Life Maturity	Convergence	Afterglow
Foundations laid through family and culture of origin, as well as life shaping events	Seeking to know God more intimately with basic supportive ministry tasks	Learning ministry skills and experiencing empowerment of gifts	Best Contribution is emerging. Ministry is "being" more than "doing".	God moves you into a role that matches your Best Contribution.	Life wisdom continues to benefit many through broad base of relationships.

Time

[315]

Phase 1	Phase 2	Phase 3	Phase 4	Phase 5
Sovereign Foundations	Inner-Life Growth	Ministry Maturing	Life Maturing	Convergence

Natural abilities	Training	Ministry	Ministry	Role matches gift-
Personality traits	Modeling	Activities	Effectiveness	mix/experience/
Spiritual gift-mix	Mentoring	from Doing	from Being	temperament
Family origin	Apprenticeship		Gift	Fullness
	Character growth		emergence	Maximum impact

---

[314] In real life, phases 3, 4 and 5 often overlap although the diagram shows them sequentially.
[315] Dr. J. Robert Clinton, *The Making of a Leader: Recognizing the Lessons and Stages of Leadership Development* (NavPress, 1988).

Determining your Life Phase

Directions: The strengths of each phase are carried forward. For example, as you begin to acquire ministry skills, which is initiated in the ministry maturity phase, your life would normally be characterized by continuing to know God more intimately which was initiated in the inner life growth phase. If you think you are between phases, or transitioning into a new phase you will find appropriate "ENTERING . . ." categories.

Remember to view "ministry" in the broadest sense without a dualistic mindset, not limiting ministry activity solely to a church context.

◯ **SOVEREIGN FOUNDATIONS:** family, environmental and historical events

◯ **ENTERING INNER LIFE:** seeker

◯ **INNER LIFE GROWTH:** seeking to know God more intimately, supportive tasks from the biblical value of service

◯ **ENTERING MINISTRY MATURITY:** accept wide range of ministry opportunities to build character and understand your gift mix

◯ **MINISTRY MATURITY:** accept wide range of ministry opportunities to build character and understand your gift mix

◯ **ENTERING LIFE MATURITY:** most ministry is

consistent with gifts within priorities but diligence is required for some responsibilities outside of gifting

◯ **LIFE MATURITY:** most ministry is consistent with gifts within priorities but diligence is required for some responsibilities outside of gifting

◯ **ENTERING CONVERGENCE:** broad recognition of spiritual authority attracts resources that enable you to function exclusively within your gifts

◯ **CONVERGENCE:** broad recognition of spiritual authority attracts resources that enable you to function exclusively within your gifts

◯ **AFTERGLOW:** celebrating and reaping the dividends of a lifetime of ministry and growth, along with passing on the mantle of your wisdom and experience to the next generation

Focus Areas

Highlight those groups and/or areas for which you have a special concern or passion, and to which you gravitate. The list below is not comprehensive so if your passion or area of calling is not listed, write in the space marked "Other."

Sphere/Domain

Education	Arts and Entertainment	Health
- College/University	- Dance	- Public health
- Post-graduate	- Music	- Healthcare
- Adult education	- Art	- Mental/psychology
- Secondary	- Theatre	- Counseling
- Pre-school	- Hollywood/Film	- Therapy
- Vocational	- Sports	- Occupational
- Philosophy	- Architecture	- Personal health
- Curriculum	- Comedy	- Nutrition
- Home-school	- Literature	- Animal health
- Character development	-	-
-	-	-
-	-	-

Media	Economy and Business	Science and technology
- Press/Journalism	- Public sector	- Environment
- National	- Private sector	- Climate change
- Local	- Employment	- Weather
- TV and Radio	- Primary/raw materials	- Biology/genetics
- Internet	- Secondary/ manufacturing	- Physics
-	- Tertiary/services	- Chemistry
-	- Management	- Earth
Family	- Sales/marketing	- Biomedical
- Parenting	- Advertising	- Epidemiology
- Child development	- Ethics	- Research
- Marriage	- Taxation	- Innovation
- Elderly	- Utilities	-
- Extended family	- Balance of trade/ national debt	-
- Widows	- Finance/banking	**Government/Politics**
- Orphans	- Stock market	- International
- Single parent	- Accounting	- National
-		- Local
-		- Legislation/Legal
-		- Judiciary/Justice

Religion	-	- Executive
- Church	-	- Armed forces
- Mission agencies	**Infrastructure**	- Prisons
- Bible schools	- Planning	-
- X-cultural mission	- Telecommunications	**Agriculture**
- Other faiths	- Transportation	- Land management
- Poor and needy	- Energy	- Forestry
- Homeless	- Water management	- Animal husbandry
-	-	- Organic farming
Social/Non-profit	-	- Agricultural science
- Humanitarian	-	- Factory farming
- Relief and development	-	- Free range
- Charities		- Sustainable agriculture
- NGO's		- Urban agriculture
- Foundations		-
-		-
-		Other: _____
-		-
-		-

People Groups

Age	Cultural/Geographic	People Needs
Infants	Extended family	Deaf
Pre-schoolers	Neighborhood	Blind
Children	City _____	Disabled
Teens	Nation _____	Special needs
College/university students	Internationals/diaspora	Homeless
	Region _____	Poor
Career singles	People group _____	Debt
Young marrieds	Least reached	Unemployed
Couples	Muslim	Wealthy
Young parents	Buddhist	People of public influence
Parents of teens	Hindu	
Older people	Tribal	Other: _____
Other: _____	Communist	
	Jewish	
	Women	
	Men	
	Other: _____	

Integration–Personal Profile

Use this profile to capture and draw together what you have discovered about how God has made you and for what purpose.

Calling and Life Purpose

    Calling/Purpose Statement–

    Life Phase–

Spiritual Gifts (three most dominant gifts in each category, not selecting Manifestation gifts)

    Ministry–

    Key use in the sphere of your passion–

    Motivational–

    Key use in the sphere of your passion–

    Gift mix–

Heart and Passion (key insights from questions related to what motivates and drives you)

    Sphere of society/influence most drawn to–

Abilities and Talents (key discoveries from natural ability profile)

    Key use in the sphere of your passion–

Personality

    DISC–

    MBTI–

    Enneagram–

    Personality description–

Experience (key insights for each area)

    Family experiences–

    Educational experiences–

    Vocational experiences–

Spiritual experiences–

Ministry experiences–

Painful experiences–

Relational experiences–

Significant events/turning points in your life–

How the above can be used to advance the kingdom of God–

Key use in the sphere of your passion–

Vocational Bible Study

For illustrative purposes and to help inspire you to study your occupational sphere, here is an example from a Study Guide produced by the Disciple Nations Alliance. Information on advanced and more detailed study to further assist you connect your vocation with the kingdom of God can also be found on the website of the Disciple Nations Alliance.[316]

Explanatory notes:

Nature of God: Offers insight on that part of God's character from which the vocation may be framed.

Foundation verse: Offers a potential starting point for exploring the vocation.

Discovery verses: Identifies a few representative verses found in scripture that may help to shape our vocational understanding. The verses used in the Discovery section are a small starting point.

They are representative, not exhaustive.

Vocational insight: Provides a place to write any insights you gain from the passage. One of the boxes is filled in as an example of a potential insight.

Questions for further reflection and application: Provides a place to answer the question, "How am I going to apply what I am learning?" It is a place to record questions the passage raises on which you may want to further reflect. Again, an example is presented.

Quote: Provides an insight related to the vocation.

---

[316] www.disciplenations.org.

As you study, pray and ask God to open your eyes of understanding as to how the truth of scripture may speak into your vocation.

As you look up the Discovery verses, ask questions of the text in the following order:

1. What does it say? (Hear the text!)

Look for new insights about God, man, and creation as they relate to your vocation. Look at both individual "trees" as well as the larger "forest."

2. What does it mean? (What light does this shed on my occupation?)

Look for both principles and for technical knowledge.

3. How does it apply? (What am I going to do with this?)

What does God want me to do with this as it relates to my vocation? The passage itself may raise questions in your own mind that require further reflection. Those may be recorded in the column labeled "Questions for Further Reflection and Application."

AGRICULTURE

(Farmer, gardener, horticulturalist, rancher, agronomist, forester)

Nature of God: Horticulturalist. God was the first farmer; he planted the first garden.

Foundation verse: *"The LORD God took the man and put him in the Garden of Eden to work it and take care of it." Genesis 2:15*

Discovery verses	Vocational Insight	Questions for Further Reflection and Application
Genesis 1:28–30		
Genesis 2:8–9a	Who was the first farmer? God was a gardener. If the God of the universe was a "farmer," this must be a very worthy vocation.	How can we practically help farmers come to understand/see that their vocation is a very worthy and godly one?

Discovery verses	Vocational Insight	Questions for Further Reflection and Application
Genesis 3:17–18		
Leviticus 19:9–10		
Psalm 80:8–19		
Proverbs 6:6–11		
Proverbs 24:30–34		
Isaiah 24:4–5		
Mark 4:1–20		
Mark 4:30–32		
John 15:1–8		
Revelation 22:1–2		

Empowered! Discovering Your Place in God's Story

> The creation story, the creation of the world. "In the beginning God…created the heavens and the earth….and God said, Behold, I have given you every herb yielding seed, which is upon the face of all the earth, and every tree, in which is the fruit of a tree yielding seed; to you it shall be for food:…"
>
> "Behold" there means "look," "search," "find out"… That to me is the most wonderful thing of life.
>
> Responding to the inquiry of an agricultural journalist as to how he had gone about his exploration of the peanut and its uses, Carver replied, "Why, I just took a handful of peanuts and looked at them. "Great Creator," I said, *why* did you make the peanut? Why?"
>
> With such knowledge as I had of chemistry and physics I set to work to take the peanut apart. I separated the water, the fats, the oils, the gums, the resins, sugars, starches, pectoses, and amedo acids. There! I had the parts of the peanut all spread out before me. Then I merely went on to try different combinations of those parts, under different conditions of temperature, pressure, and so forth.
>
> The result was what you see—these 202 different products, all made from peanuts!

317

Note

George Washington Carver is credited as one of the first advocates of sustainable agriculture and organic fertilizing techniques and for making known hundreds of practical uses for products derived from the peanut, sweet potato, pecan, and clay. Though popularly remembered for inventing hundreds of peanut-based products, Carver accomplished much, much more.

---

[317] George Washington Carver, in John S. Ferrel, *Fruits of Creation* (Austin, Minn.: Macalaster Park Publishing Company, 1995), 62, 50.

BIBLIOGRAPHY

Allen, Roland. *Missionary Methods: St. Paul's or Ours?* Wm. B. Eerdmans Publishing, 1912, 1962

Barna, George. *Revolution,* Tyndale House Publishers, 2005

Barna, George with Mark Hatch. *Boiling Point: Monitoring Cultural Shifts in the 21st Century,* Regal Publishing, 2003

Beck, James R. *Dorothy Carey: The Tragic and Untold Story of Mrs William Carey,* Baker Book House, 1992

Beckham, William A. *The Second Reformation: Reshaping the Church for the 21st Century,* Touch Publications, 1995

Brown, Alistair. *I Believe in Mission,* Hodder and Stoughton, 1997

Careaga, Andrew. *eMinistry: Connecting with the Net Generation,* Kregel Academic and Professional, 2001

Clinton, Dr. J. Robert. *The Making of a Leader: Recognizing the Lessons and Stages of Leadership Development,* NavPress, 1988

Cope, Landa. *An Introduction to The Old Testament Template: Rediscovering God's Principles for Discipling Nations,* The Template Institute Press, 2006

Coleman, Robert E. *The Master Plan of Evangelism,* Revell Publishing, 1963, 1964, 1993

Crossman, Meg, ed. *Worldwide Perspectives: Biblical, Historical, Strategic, and Cultural Dimensions of God's Plan for the Nations,* YWAM Publishing, 2003

Cunningham, Loren. *Is That Really You, God?* Grand Rapids, MI: Chosen Books, 1984

_____ with Janice Rogers. *The Book that Transforms Nations: The Power of the Bible to Change Any Country,* YWAM Publishing, 2007

Eldredge, John. *Waking the Dead: The Glory of a Heart Fully Alive,* Thomas Nelson Publishers, 2003

Ferrel, John S. *Fruits of Creation,* Austin, Minn: Macalaster Park Publishing Co., 1995

Frost, Michael and Alan Hirsch, *The Shaping of Things to Come,* Peabody: Hendrickson, 2003

Greene, Mark. *Supporting Christians at Work,* Administry and LICC Publications, 2001

Guder, Darrel L., ed. *Missional Church: A Vision for the Sending of the Church in North America,* Grand Rapids: Eerdmans, 1998

_____. *The Continuing Conversion of the Church,* Wm. B. Eerdmans Publishing Co., 2000

Guinness, Os. *The Call: Finding and Fulfilling the Central Purpose of Your Life,* W Publishing Group, 1998, 2003

Hampton, Michael. *Head versus Heart and our Gut Reaction: The 21st Century Enneagram,* O Books Publishing, 2005

Hegeman, David Bruce. *Plowing in Hope: Toward a Biblical Theology of Culture,* Canon Press, 1999

Hillman, Os. *The 9 to 5 Window: How Faith can Transform the Workplace,* Regal Books, 2005

Hirsch, Alan and Debra Hirsch. *Untamed: Reactivating a Missional Form of Discipleship,* Baker Books, 2010

Hirsch, Alan and Ford, Lance. *Right Here, Right Now: Everyday Mission for Everyday People,* Baker Books, 2011

Holzmann, John, ed. *The Church of the East,* Sonlight Curriculum Publishing, 2001

Jacobs, Cindy. *The Reformation Manifesto: Your Part in God's Plan to Change Nations Today,* Bethany House Publishing, 2008

Johnson, Todd M. and Kenneth R. Ross, eds. *Atlas of Global Christianity,* Edinburgh University Press, 2009

Kelly, Gerard. *Stretch: Lessons in Faith from the Life of Daniel,* Authentic Publishing, 2005

Kinoti, George. *Hope for Africa and What the Christian Can Do,* African Institute for Scientific Research and Development, 1994

Lanier, Sarah. *Foreign to Familiar: A Guide to Understanding Hot- and Cold-Climate Cultures,* McDougal Publishing, 2000

Law, Eric. *The Wolf Shall Dwell with the Lamb,* Chalice Press, 1993

Lawrence, Brother. *Practicing the Presence of God,* Revell Publishing, reprinted ed., 1967

Lewis, C.S. *The Last Battle,* Harper Collins, 1956, 1999

Mandryk, Jason. *Operation World: The Definitive Prayer Guide to Every Nation,* Biblica Publishing, 2010

Mangalwadi, Vishal. *The Book that Made Your World: How the Bible Created the Soul of Western Civilization,* Thomas Nelson, 2011

_____. *Truth and Transformation: A Manifesto for Ailing Nations,* YWAM Publishing, 2009

Mangalwadi, Ruth and Vishal Mangalwadi. *The Legacy of William Carey: A Model for the Transformation of a Culture,* Crossway Books, 1999

McGavran, Donald A. *The Bridges of God: A Study in the Strategy of Missions.* Wipf and Stock Publishers, new edition, 1955, 2005

_____. *Understanding Church Growth.* Wm B. Eerdmans Publishing Company, 3rd edition, 1990

Miller, Darrow L. *My Place in HIStory: Discovering Your Calling,* Disciple Nations Alliance, 2009

Miller, Darrow L. with Scott Allen and the African Working Group of Samaritan Strategy Africa. *Against All Hope: Hope for Africa,* Disciple Nations Alliance, Inc., 2005

Miller, Darrow L. with Stan Guthie, Stan. *Discipling Nations: The Power of Truth to Transform Cultures,* YWAM Publishing, 1998, 2001

_____. *Nurturing the Nations: Reclaiming the Dignity of Women in Building Healthy Cultures,* Paternoster Publishing, 2008

Miller, Darrow L. with Newton, Marit. *LifeWork: A Biblical Theology for What You Do Every Day,* YWAM Publilshing, 2009

Moffitt, Bob. *If Jesus were Mayor: Biblical and Historical Roots of Cultural Transformation through the Church,* Harvest Foundation, 2005

Morris, Linus J. *The High Impact Church: A Fresh Approach to Reaching the Unreached,* Gospel Light, 1993

Newbigin, Lesslie. *Foolishness to the Greeks: The Gospel and Western Culture,* Wm. B. Eerdmans Publishing, 1986

_____. *The Open Secret: An Introduction to the Theology of Missions,* Wm. B. Eerdmans Publishing, 1978, 1995

Olson, C. Godon. *What in the World is God Doing? The Essentials of Global Missions: An Introductory Guide,* Global Gospel Publications, 4th edition, 2001

Peabody, Larry. *Job-Shadowing Daniel: Walking the Talk at Work,* Outskirts Press, 2010

_____. *Secular Work is Full-Time Service* (re-titled *Serving Christ in the Workplace*), Christian Literature Crusade, 1980, 2004

Pearcey, Nancy. *Total Truth: Liberating Christianity from its Cultural Captivity,* Crossway Books, 2004

Pirolo, Neal. *Serving as Senders: How to Care for your Missionaries While They are Preparing to Go, While They are on the Field, When They are Home,* Emmaus Road International, 1991

Rohr, Richard and Andreas Ebert, *The Enneagram: A Christian Perspective,* Crossroads Publications, 2001

Roxburgh, Alan J. and M. Scott Boren, *Introducing the Missional Church: What it is, Why it Matters, How to Become One,* Baker Books, 2009

Schaeffer, Francis. *The Mark of a Christian.* Norfolk Press, 1970

Sider, Ronald J., ed. *Evangelicals and Development: Towards a Theology of Social Change,* Philadelphia: Westminster Press, 1981

Stark, Rodney. *The Rise of Christianity: How the Obscure, Marginal, Jesus Movement Became the Dominant Religious Force,* Harper Collins Publishers, 1997

_____ *The Victory of Reason: How Christianity Led to Freedom, Capitalism and Western Success,* Random House Publishing Group, 2005

Stier, Jim, Richlyn Poor and Lisa Orvis, eds. *His Kingdom Come–An Integrated Approach to Discipling the Nations and Fulfilling the Great Commission,* YWAM Publishing, 2008

Snyder, Howard. The Community of the King, Inter-Varsity Press, 1977

Taylor, Dr. and Mrs Howard. *Hudson Taylor's Spiritual Secret,* Moody Publishers, 1955, 2009

Taylor, J. Hudson. *China's Spiritual Need and Claims,* Morgan and Scott, 1865, 1887

Taylor, William D., ed. *Global Missiology for the 21st Century,* Grand Rapids: Baker Academic, 2000

_____. ed. *Too Valuable to Lose: Exploring the Causes and Cures of Missionary Attrition,* William Carey Library, 1997

Tenney, Tommy. *God's Dream Team–A Call to Unity,* Regal Books, 1999

Tiplady, Richard. *World of Difference: Global Mission at the Pic "N" Mix Counter,* Paternoster Press, 2003

Viola, Frank and George Barna. *Pagan Christianity? Exploring the Roots of our Church Practices,* Barna Books, 2008

Warren, Rick. *The Purpose Driven Life,* Zondervan Publishing, 2002

Weber, Max. *The Protestant Ethic and the Spirit of Capitalism,* Scribner Library, New York, 1958

Winter, Ralph D., and Steven C. Hawthorne, eds. *Perspectives on the World Christian Movement: A Reader.* 4th ed. Pasadena: William Carey Library, 2009

Yohannan, K. P. *Revolution in World Missions,* Gospel for Asia Books, 1986

Yun, Brother with Paul Hattaway, *The Heavenly Man: The Remarkable Story of Chinese Christian Brother Yun,* Monarch Books, 2002

ADDITIONAL RESOURCES

Websites:
Biblical Worldview Institute–aims to impact the culture by equipping educators from the school, the home, and the church, with the ability to show students of all ages how to apply biblical truth into all of life.
www.biblicalworldviewinstitute.org

Call2All–a worldwide movement calling the church to a renewed, focused collaborative effort to complete the Great Commission.
www.call2all.org

Disciple Nations Alliance–a global movement seeking to equip the church to transform the world.
www.disciplenations.org www.MondayChurch.org

Empower Coaching–the author's coaching website with information on life coaching and various assessment tools to help individuals discover their God-given design.
www.stuartmsimpson.com

Marketplace Institute, Regent College—a public theology think tank that exists to support and promote the transformational impact of the Christian faith throughout all aspects of modern life. It does so by engaging directly in the public marketplace of ideas and debate, and by equipping and envisioning Christians and churches in their varied vocations in society.
www.regent-college.edu/marketplace

Marketplace Leaders–a ministry to help men and women fulfill God's call on their lives by understanding the role faith plays in their workplace calling.
    www.marketplaceleaders.org

Newforms Resources–a training and resource company that serves church planting movements, churches in transition and simple/organic/missional communities, and engagement in kingdom mission.
    www.newformsresources.com

The London Institute of Contemporary Christianity–seeks to envision and equip Christians and churches for whole-life discipleship in the world.
    www.licc.org.uk

The Template Institute–seeks to facilitate biblical thinking in the professions and public arenas.
    www.templateinstitute.com

Vishal Mangalwadi–an international lecturer, social reformer, political columnist and author.
    www.revelationmovement.com

QUESTIONS FOR REFLECTION OR DISCUSSION

Chapter 1

1. How does a biblically-informed worldview affect our view of history?

2. How would you describe God's Mission Statement?

3. How does your worldview reflect your understanding of the Great Commission?

4. Do you feel connected or disconnected to the Great Commission mandate? If you feel disconnected, why do you think that is?

Chapter 2

1. Why is a return to a belief in absolute truth based on God's Word essential to disciple our families, communities, and nations?

2. Explain why the Christian faith is not having the influence that it should in the societies, cultures and nations where it is in evidence?

3. Noting how the Bible (eg. in Deuteronomy 28) describes a blessed nation, how do you

think God views the state of your people/country?

4. The chapter includes the following quote by Dr. Adeyemo, "I salute the early missionaries who came to us, but often the gospel did not get beyond skin deep because it did not transform our traditional worldview." How do you understand what is being said in respect to the spread of Christianity in much of Africa today?

5. A diluted and dualistic worldview has robbed many believers of the joy of knowing that they had a unique contribution to make to the kingdom of God. Do you feel you have been affected by the Spiritual-Secular divide? If so, how?

6. What new paradigms will be required within the Fourth Wave for engaging in God's mission?

Chapter 3

1. Discuss the danger of losing sight of the big picture and the main storyline of what God is doing.

2. Explain the difference between the gospel of the kingdom and the gospel of salvation.

3. Share your understanding of the kingdom of God.

Chapter 4

1. Explain the two components of the Great Commission mandate.

2. How is a nation discipled?

3. Consider which of the spheres of society you are called to or feel drawn towards. How might you bring a transforming influence into those areas of society?

4. How has this chapter expanded your vision of God?

Chapter 5

1. Is God's Mission the core operating principle for your life and the life of your local church? If not, how might this change?

2. "Christians, churches, and mission organizations must be willing to be perceived as "trouble-makers" or counter-culture." Explain the tension between not adapting and conforming to culture, but representing kingdom culture in a relevant way *within* our existing culture.

3. How do you understand living a missional lifestyle?

Chapter 6

1. Do you have a lifestyle that is lived *coram Deo* (or before the audience of One)? How might this affect how you view engaging with the Great Commission mandate?

2. Where do you see yourself in the Living in ONE World diagram? Do you feel released in your vocation and calling when you adopt a biblical frame of reference rather than a dualistic paradigm?

3. What is your current mission field or place of deployment?

Chapter 7

1. Do you see yourself as being called to God's ministry?

2. How have church practices of ordination perpetuated the "clergy-laity," "spiritual-secular" divisions and reinforced the idea that only some Christians are called to ministry?

3. What impact would it make in your life if you were publicly commissioned into your calling and sphere(s) of influence in society? How might this impact the life of your church if every believer in your local church community were prayed for and sent out?

Chapter 8

1. Do you feel equipped for what God has called you to?

2. How much vocation-related teaching from the Bible have you received?

3. What opportunities do you have to engage in *diaspora* ministry? How can you be better equipped to be more effective in this area?

4. Are you involved in supporting a missionary (or missionaries)? How can you help them be more effective in the work God has called them to?

5. How is new technology equipping Christians to complete the task of the Great Commission?

Chapter 9

1. What are you living for?

2. Do you know your life purpose? Why do you think God put you on the earth?

3. How might a vision of God's future kingdom on earth impact how you live your life today?

4. What "causes" are you passionate about?

5. How has God invested in your life? How might He be expecting you to steward what He has entrusted you with?

Chapter 10

1. How much do you already know about your God-given SHAPE and design? What will you do to get a better understanding of who God has made you?

2. Choose one of the five key factors that make up your SHAPE and reflect on (or share) what God has shown you. Pray over the key insights you have received.

3. Create a personal mission (calling) statement, and/or vision board.

Chapter 11

1. Reflect (share) on how an area of culture and society has been influenced away from a biblical worldview. How might a biblical influence and transformation be brought about?

2. Which of the present-day illustrations inspired you and why? How can you begin to live out your own missional story?

3. How can you be intentional in using your God-given gifts, abilities and passions to bring a godly influence and work towards an advancement of God's kingdom on earth?

About the Author

Stuart Simpson (D.Min) is an apostolic teacher, author, and coach. He and his wife, Michelle, are the co-founders of Catalyst Ministries and long-time missionaries with Youth With A Mission. After more than 20 years in pioneer missions in China and Thailand, including four years in Chinese student ministry in England, two years in Canada and three years in the USA, Stuart is currently based in the UK. He is the author of several books, including *The Second Act: The Remarkable Story of Missionary James O. Fraser's 'Successor' & Key Lessons for Mission Work Today*, and *Kingdom Mission: A Call to Disciple Nations* (co-authored with Peter J. Farmer). He also acted the leading role in the gold remi award winning docudrama produced by OMF International: *Breakthrough: The Life of James O. Fraser and the Lisu People.*

    Stuart is trained in life coaching and administering the Highlands Ability Battery, and other assessments related to personal development and missionary team health. Through coaching and training, Stuart empowers believers and churches to engage in the full scope of the Great Commission, including the mandate to disciple nations. He has a doctorate in ministry, with a specialization in cross-cultural and kingdom mission.

Web: www.catalystmin.org
& www.stuartmsimpson.com
Email: catalystmin@gmail.com
empowercoach7@gmail.com

Printed in Great Britain
by Amazon